For years, my students and I have looked at dedication pages with puzzlement. Just who are those people? we would wonder. Now I know.

This book is dedicated to my mother, who encouraged our childhood dramatic play, and to the teachers, teaching artists, and students with whom these techniques were developed and refined.

Contents

Active Learning Through Drama, Podcasting, and Puppetry

Kristin Fontichiaro

LIBRARIES

U N L I M I T E D

A Member of the Greenwood Publishing Group

Westport, Connecticut • London

Library of Congress Cataloging-in-Publication Data

Fontichiaro, Kristin.
　Active learning through drama, podcasting and puppetry / Kristin Fontichiaro.
　p. cm.
　Includes bibliographical references and index.
　ISBN-13: 978–1–59158–402–5 (alk. paper)
　ISBN-10: 1–59158–402–7 (alk. paper)
　1. Creative activities and seat work. 2. Instructional materials centers. 3. Arts—Study and teaching (Elementary) I. Title.
　LB1537.F64 2007
　372.66—dc22　2006036842

British Library Cataloguing in Publication Data is available.

Library of Congress Catalog Card Number: 2006036842
ISBN: 978–1–59158–402–5

First published in 2007

Libraries Unlimited, 88 Post Road West, Westport, CT 06881
A Member of the Greenwood Publishing Group, Inc.
www.lu.com

Printed in the United States of America

∞™

The paper used in this book complies with the
Permanent Paper Standard issued by the National
Information Standards Organization (Z39.48–1984).

10 9 8 7 6 5 4 3 2 1

Acknowledgments

All teachers and performing artists are shaped by those who have guided them. I am lucky to have a long list and a forum with which to share them.

To my family, who encouraged role play and creative drama at home, I am grateful. My mother's linen closet, which seemed to have an endless supply of bedsheets for us to convert into backdrops, costumes, and scenery, provided inspiration for years. My father's educational experience set high standards for my work as an educator. My grandmother, Ailie Wappula, took pride in my theatrical interest, saying it was genetic: her relatives had performed pro-Prohibition plays in Michigan's Upper Peninsula.

Jackie Plas and Anna Giddings of the Walled Lake Consolidated Schools gave me my first introduction to improvisational drama as a student, and the joy of those experiences resonates with me when I pass those ideas on to my own students. I am grateful to the staff and faculty of the University of Michigan and University Productions for grounding me in theatrical principles.

Jane Walters and the Craigmont Middle/High School staff encouraged me to take the leap from professional stage management to education and provided a model of how the arts could motivate and excite a diverse student population. Melissa Cychowski was the first art teacher with whom I felt the power of collaboration; her friendship and professional generosity guided me in my first attempt to create a performance text from a picture book, along with my first time making Styrofoam™ scenery. The staff of St. Mary's Episcopal School in Memphis, Tennessee, gave me a teaching home that embraced the arts and celebrated the student as artist.

My colleagues at the University Musical Society, especially Ken Fischer, Ben Johnson, and Warren Williams, gave me opportunities to work as a teaching artist, workshop leader, and arts education manager. Our visiting teaching artists from the Kennedy Center, including Susan Griss, Michele Valeri, Lenore Blank Kelner, and Sean Layne, were instrumental in shaping my vision for arts-integrated education. Mary Johnson, Virginia Grainger, and the late Clare Venables of the Royal Shakespeare Company modeled assertive teaching and taught me so much about the power of improvisational drama to decipher text. Lynda Berg of the Ann Arbor Public Schools remains a terrific friend and sounding board, a superb blending of artistic vision and practical sensibility. I learned a great deal about advocacy from her.

Gail Trapp Bohner, Brenda Gluth, Erin Dahl, and I worked together to create the framework for the Brighton Area Schools' first SMART Camp, a two-week summer shadow puppetry camp. Many of the SMART Camp strategies are included in the shadow puppetry chapter of this book, with grateful thanks.

Jan Toth-Chernin of Greenhills School taught me that librarians could be vibrant and creative and still provide great service. Dian Walster of Wayne State University helped me articulate my role as media specialist and helped with advocacy. Linda Ligon, my practicum supervisor at Winston Churchill High School, encouraged me to seek employment that would satisfy my creative tendencies.

Kay Nicholas at the Miller Early Childhood Center made it possible for me to have a year experimenting with shaping the "circle drama" technique with kindergarten students. Where else could I have tried *The Mitten* 25 times in a two-week period? Sarah Credo at Hawkins Elementary was my partner in crime during the first *Very Quiet Cricket* project. Diane Plath's classroom was the birthplace of the assembly line drama machine described in this book.

Ron Stowe and Donna Power of the Institute for Education and the Arts gave me a chance to grow as an arts educator, consultant, and advocate.

Greg Strom, my teaching partner with the American Professional Partnership for Lithuanian Education (A.P.P.L.E.), documented much of our arts integration seminar with Lithuanian teachers, which became a valuable resource during the writing of this book. Our 2005 course participants taught me a great deal about pushing the limits of shadow puppetry.

Blanche Woolls, my A.P.P.L.E. colleague, first envisioned this book during a bus ride in Vilnius. Sharon Coatney provided insights that improved this book and my practice as a media specialist. Laurie Cooper, Julie de Klerk, Chris Fontichiaro, Kerry Fontichiaro, Maja Fontichiaro, Rob Fontichiaro, Sue Kohfeldt, Mark Nelson, Kim O'Rourke, and Vicki Pascaretti read drafts of this book and offered valuable insights.

Barbara Jones-Clark and Jennifer Martella of the Birmingham Public Schools gave me a home as media specialist at Beverly School, where I have continued to grow as a teaching librarian. Jacquie Stephenson's expertise and good humor are invaluable.

To all the teachers and students who helped me refine these techniques over the years, thank you.

Introduction

Imagine your media center alive with energy as students actively engage with books and research. Imagine that, while the quality of their work deepens, the number of behavior management issues decreases. These are just some of the benefits of integrating drama lessons into the media center curriculum.

This book explores several techniques for bringing the arts into children's daily learning, paying particular attention to classroom management, tapping into students' intrinsic motivation, and using the arts to explore and assess student learning. This is a book about creative learning, about energizing the media center and motivating K–8 students toward greater comprehension and understanding. Learning academic content through drama—though improvisation, performance, and puppetry—is deeply satisfying for media specialists and their students. Media centers come alive as students use their bodies, voices, imagination, concentration, and cooperation to interact with and showcase learning about literature and research topics. By scaffolding activities and building drama skills alongside the academic content, students gain artistic skills and content area success.

This book is a reflection of my growing work and practice as a teacher, teaching artist, and librarian, focusing on three primary areas: improvisational drama, voice work, and shadow puppetry. These techniques have been field-tested in my media center (though they work equally well in the classroom), and they *work*. Students are excited to learn and to show what they have learned.

■ HOW IT BEGAN

For me, teaching through the performing arts in the media center began accidentally. A small group of kindergarten students had come to the media center to learn about the rain cycle. We looked through Gail Saunders-Smith's book *Rain* (Pebble Books, 1998). I read the text aloud, and the students and I discussed the text and pictures.

"So," I said, closing the book, "What are you going to tell your class about how rain works?" I expected them to repeat the water cycle back to me. After all, we had talked about it and looked at it, right? That's what had worked for the other groups of kindergarteners.

Instead, I got blank stares. Finally, one girl spoke up timidly: "I don't get it."

"Well," I said, "it's kind of like this." Without thinking, I began to use my hands to show how the vapor rose up into the clouds, which held the vapor until there was too much tension. "And then," I said, holding my fists tightly in front of me, "the clouds say, 'I CAN'T STAND IT ANYMORE!' because there's too much water in the clouds, and it rains." We repeated the finger play together.

I saw the gleam of recognition in their eyes. *Now* they understood the water cycle. We had used our voices and our bodies to animate the water cycle. Our bodies had shown us that vapors traveled upward, while the rain came down. Our voices, shouting, "I JUST CAN'T STAND IT ANYMORE!" reinforced the tension "felt" in the clouds before rain was released. These kindergarteners hadn't learned by sitting around the table. They wanted to *move* and *experience* things. Through that movement and experience, they had learned.

When the children returned to the classroom, their teacher said, "What did you learn?" and the children broke into the water cycle drama, shouting out, "I JUST CAN'T STAND IT ANYMORE!" and grinning sheepishly at the end.

Twenty minutes. That was it. From start to finish, only 20 minutes had passed. Had we met the classroom teacher's objective—to understand rain's role in the water cycle? Absolutely.

This is what we all do as teachers. We see a teachable moment, invent a way of teaching it on the spot, and are sometimes surprised and delighted by what happens. I picked up the next research group and headed back to the media center. This group was going to study fog. This would be easy, right? Just look at the pictures, read a few words, and report back to class.

As before, we went through the book and studied the photographs. We talked about times when we had been on foggy roads and how parents had slowed down their cars. We talked about how sometimes we had indoor recess if it was too foggy.

"But when are we going to do our play?" said one girl. Play? We weren't here to do a play, I thought. *We were here to learn about fog.*

"Yes, how are we going to act out fog?" said her classmate. How, indeed? I thought. Frankly, I had no idea; I just knew we had five minutes to complete this research lesson. So I asked them.

"How would *you* act out fog?"

The girl said, "I'd stand like *this*." She stood up straight, feet wide apart, arms spread wide. In a booming voice, she said, "I AM FOG. I make it HARD for people to SEE." The others instantly fell into line with her, a line of fog.

This is when the light bulb clicked for me. We had just used the performing arts to *explore* content and to *demonstrate* what we had learned. Drama hadn't been tangential to these weather projects; it hadn't been an enrichment activity; it hadn't been prescripted, preplanned, or prepackaged. It had been the gateway that had allowed children to engage in and share their knowledge.

Looking back, I'm surprised that it took me this long. I have an undergraduate degree in theatre, have worked professionally as a stage manager, coordinated several arts education partnership activities while a middle school language arts teacher, and spent three years managing a K–12 arts education program. But somehow, these simple truths—that the performing arts help us interact and make meaning from content and that the arts also help us show what we've learned *in the library*—never hit home as well as they did that day, when arts-based learning had worked in my library when more traditional instructional methods had not.

I thought back to the teacher workshops we had sponsored when I had managed the Youth Education Program at the University Musical Society of the University of Michigan. I had been exposed to some of the finest educators in arts-integrated education, teaching artists from the Kennedy Center Partners in Education Program, Juilliard, and the Royal Shakespeare Company.

As I grew as a media specialist, I continued to find ways to incorporate arts education into the media center curriculum, adapting techniques to fit my time constraints and the school district's teaching and learning objectives. I looked for authentic connections among drama, puppetry, and the school library. I wasn't interested in activities that were "cute" but disconnected from the curriculum. I wasn't interested in doing drama that was wild or out of control or in simplistic lesson plans that consisted solely of the sentence, "Now have your students act this out," without any strategies for how to do that effectively. I was looking for *resonance*—lessons and projects providing *deep learning opportunities.*

Word of the rain and fog "plays" reached my then-principal. She asked me to use drama as a key teaching strategy in the media center. At the time, I was half-time in an all-kindergarten building—25 classes of kindergarteners! What a laboratory. Many of the early childhood lessons in this book had their genesis during that time.

In addition to the all-kindergarten building, I taught half-time in an elementary school library. There, I began to introduce drama and puppetry techniques as a way of building on curriculum objectives—not as separate activities but as activities that contributed to students' understanding of core knowledge.

With practice, my techniques improved, and my "role" as teacher/director/coaxer became more natural. I began to structure the lessons more effectively, incorporating a variety of warm-up activities that prepared students better for the drama experience. Drama and puppetry evolved as natural frameworks for interesting, engaging, high-level learning. I learned how, when a performance activity is the goal, it calls on children to interact in new ways with information, generating new learning. The performing arts also served as superb motivators, keeping students engaged more deeply and for a longer period of time. The arts also helped me naturally differentiate instruction for students with special needs; often, students who are weak readers or writers are energized when they can demonstrate their understanding through the methods described in this book.

I am grateful for my current position, where our media center is well-staffed and well-supported, and has plenty of open space and flexible schedule time for dramatic experimentation. Our media center is a creative learning center for the school, a place where a visitor is as likely to find children creating a clay animation film as creating a historical fiction shadow puppet play to show their understanding of the Transcontinental Railroad. Arts-based learning is active learning, and our media center is full of activity.

ABOUT THIS BOOK

Each chapter of this book focuses on a different performing arts technique, identifying which grade levels will benefit most from each approach. Included in each chapter is a detailed description of how to make the activity work: the scaffolding, special vocabulary, techniques, and tips that dig deep into the lesson and contribute to its success. Some techniques work best as responses to storytime; others are best suited when paired with a research project. Some techniques work in either situation, and sometimes different techniques can be combined for even more impact. For example, choral readings can be experienced as artistic endeavors on their own, or they can be combined with a shadow play. Lessons learned during the composition of a dramatic tableau can also help students arrange puppets more effectively onstage.

Lesson Plans

Each section includes several sample lesson plans that work with a given technique. Some focus on literature; others are conducive to research and information literacy. Each lesson plan includes strategies to help you create the most successful experience possible. The author and illustrator index can help you find a good last-minute lesson that matches a book already in the school library.

Performance Strategies

Many lessons in this book—such as narrative pantomime and "circle drama"—focus primarily on *improvisation* and *process. Improvisation* is unplanned, spontaneous, on-the-spot artistic creation. *Process-oriented work* is concerned more with the experiential learning, the quality of discovery that is happening in the moment, than with repetition or rehearsals aimed toward a final product or performance. By keeping the focus on the improvisational period, the media specialist and collaborating teachers can capture the theatrical process at its most creative, when students are having the highest level of interaction with the academic content. The spontaneous quality of these projects makes them particularly well suited to young learners.

Other lessons in this book, such as the wax museum, radio play podcast, and shadow puppetry, are more focused on *performance,* on creating a culminating product that demonstrates what *has been learned.* These projects are useful as end-unit assessments and as alternatives to traditional written reports. Student performances are powerful for the students involved and can be formative experiences for young audiences.

Advocacy

The book concludes with a section on advocacy. Education's priorities are constantly shifting, and an artistic approach to teaching has sometimes been misinterpreted as frivolous and, therefore, in jeopardy of elimination. It is more important than ever to share, document, and articulate the quality of learning that goes on in media centers. The benefits of arts-based learning can be difficult to articulate or quantify, especially in the context of a school library. The advocacy chapter gives advice on how to showcase the benefits of arts-centered learning in the media center.

■ WEB LINKS

Please visit www.chiaroweb.com/book. There, you'll find links to historical information, additional pedagogical techniques, and further information.

■ CONCLUSION

The arts *are* powerful: they transform us and allow us to see the world in new ways. They allow us to share with others. When we harness this power by partnering the arts with curriculum content, investing time in building arts skills just as we build information literacy or math skills, we motivate our students and arm them so they can have deeper and more expressive levels of learning.

Part I
Drama

Chapter 1
The Benefits of Learning Through the Arts

■ INTRODUCTION

I was once given a cartoon that had been duplicated so many times I could no longer read the signature on it. The cartoon shows a room full of young children playing in a classroom, each with a word bubble above his or her head. A child with blocks has a bubble that reads something like, "I'm learning to sequence." Two children playing together have thought bubbles revealing, "We're learning important socialization skills." A child in the dress-up area has a bubble that reads something akin to, "I'm learning about characterization." But the two adult visitors standing at the classroom door are dumbfounded. Their word bubble reads something like, "There's no learning going on here—they're just playing!" (If anyone knows the source of this cartoon, please let me know—I'd love to give credit.)

This cartoon illustrates the central theme of this book: that arts-integrated lessons are not only fun but have significant academic, social, and workforce benefits.

This book focuses on using drama as an instructional tool and on integrating drama skills into curriculum areas of study. This process is referred to as arts-integrated education. This chapter explores some of the research-proven benefits of learning through the arts. Finally, it explores why arts integration is so important to the future of our technology-driven, global society.

■ WHAT IS ARTS-INTEGRATED LEARNING?

Arts-integrated learning is a conscious choice to teach artistic skills *in conjunction with* academic content. Sometimes led collaboratively, sometimes led by a single instructor, arts-integrated learning recognizes the value of process, not just performance. Arts-integrated learning supersedes, "Now act it out," instead scaffolding lesson plans so that students have the drama skills to bring a scene to life. Process can be as important as performance. Experiential learning is valued as much as performance-oriented learning.

As an example, consider a librarian preparing to host a Mock Caldecott contest. (The Caldecott Medal is awarded annually by the Association of Library Services to Children branch of the American Library Association for outstanding children's book illustration.) The academic content to be explored in a Mock Caldecott lesson would be the criteria for Caldecott awards and an examination of previous Caldecott winners. To make this an arts-integrated lesson plan, however, the school librarian would bring the arts curriculum into the lesson, perhaps by discussing line, shape, media, or composition (ideally, in partnership with an art teacher). By defining and using real arts terms in the lesson, students gain real-world vocabulary with which to discuss and evaluate picture books. By spending time with these definitions and discussing illustrations with these definitions, the lesson moves into an arts-integrated one. Similarly, this book's drama, voice, and puppetry activities marry academic content with artistic skills. The results are much more powerful and three-dimensional.

■ RESEARCH

Research studies show what educators and teaching artists have known for years: that the arts have a profound effect that reaches far beyond the stage, art studio, or rehearsal hall.

Champions of Change

In 1999, the President's Committee on the Arts and Humanities and the Arts Education Partnership (AEP), a coalition of over 100 arts organizations, educational institutions, philanthropic organizations, and government agencies, released *Champions of Change: The Impact of the Arts on Learning* (Fiske 1999). Among its findings, the report found that:

- Students of elementary schools that integrated the arts into classroom instruction outperformed students at other schools in math.
- Students with high levels of arts participation outscored students with low levels of arts exposure.
- Although there is a link between level of arts participation and socioeconomic level, students from low-income areas benefit more from arts instruction.
- The arts help to reach students who are otherwise not engaged in school.
- By replicating the model of a working arts troupe, the arts help students know how to function in the world of work.
- Students who worked in creating operas participated more in class and with a higher level of quality of participation.
- There is a statistically significant correlation between arts involvement and a student's grades and achievement test scores.
- Arts involvement strengthens the skills necessary for high-level, complex thinking, such as the ability to synthesize information and create a new knowledge product from it.

▶ *Critical Links*

In 2002, the Arts Education Partnership published another landmark report, *Critical Links: Learning in the Arts and Student Academic and Social Development* (Deasy 2002). Like *Champions of Change, Critical Links* is a compilation of studies and research projects from a variety of researchers, with a focus on learning through the arts. Studies summarized in the *Critical Links* report found

- positive correlations between drama and the socialization and oral language skills of learning disabled students;
- improved reading comprehension when drama was used as an instructional method with fifth-grade remedial reading students (narrative pantomime, featured in this book, was among the creative drama techniques used);
- increases in kindergartners' cognitive function and developmental gains when creative play was modeled and introduced as opposed to being left to children to develop on their own;
- improved narrative writing when coupled with drama techniques that develop prewriting skills;
- higher student engagement during dramatizations than when listening to a story being read;
- higher scores in sequencing and story recall among early elementary students engaged in fantasy play; and
- higher engagement among at-risk students when engaged in arts classes versus nonarts classes.

For a summary of these and other reports, visit the Americans for the Arts' Web page, *Highlights from Key National Research on Arts Education* (http://www.americansforthearts.org/public_awareness/articles/002.asp). It summarizes research from *Champions of Change, Critical Links,* and other studies. These studies are important tools for advocating for and clarifying the use of drama and puppetry in the curriculum.

■ WHY A HIGH-TECH, GLOBAL ECONOMY STILL NEEDS THE ARTS

The arts do wonders for performers' self-examination, reflection, and exploration. They help connect us to one another. They teach us self-discipline, deadlines, creative solutions, and multiple modalities for thinking and learning. These are some of the very skills that the business world is looking for in its future workforce.

The National Governors' Association, to which all state governors have membership, has written a series of Issue Briefs on the arts. One document, *The Impact of Arts Education on Workforce Preparation* (2002), examined several research studies and concluded that schools with arts instruction improve students' achievement, support at-risk students, engage parents in the school environment, lower absenteeism, and decrease discipline problems. At the same time, arts-integrated learning prepares the future workforce to work adaptably and flexibly in cross-functional teams, exercise higher-level thinking skills, and develop the self-discipline necessary for the twenty-first-century work environment.

Alternatively, consider how the arts can rise to meet the challenge for future American workers, as outlined in Thomas J. Friedman's 2005 book *The World Is Flat.* In the age of globalization and outsourcing, Friedman suggests that America's future advantage may lie not in performing repetitive tasks but in its innate ability to create and innovate. Future American workers will need to fit into one of four categories, he argues: special, specialized, geographically focused, and flexible. *Special* workers are the elite and possess extraordinary natural gifts that entertain our global imagination (think of stellar opera singers or world-class athletes). *Specialized* workers are extraordinarily skilled workers whose training and practice make them world leaders in their field (such as doctors with highly refined specializations or engineers who specialize in safely imploding downtown buildings without disturbing those nearby). Local (*geographically focused*) workers must be nearby to provide services and therefore cannot be outsourced (consider landscape architects, child care workers, construction workers, commercial painters, or crossing guards, all of whom must be geographically located near their clients).

These three categories of workers account for only a limited percentage of American employees. What about the majority of the workforce? Friedman argues that this majority must be trained to be *flexible,* with a varied toolkit of academic, social, and technology skills. Rather than mastering a specific checklist of skills, our K–12 graduates must be able to continually meet new challenges, revise skills, evaluate the marketplace, adapt quickly, meet short-term deadlines with constantly shifting global teams, and more. The arts, because they work in "project mode," are perfect to prepare students for this vision of the global economy. In each drama exercise, students work in different teams, set new goals, adapt quickly to the assigned activity, and complete the task with firm deadlines. "The show must go on," after all!

Friedman's thoughts were echoed in another 2005 book, Daniel H. Pink's *A Whole New Mind: Moving from the Information Age to the Conceptual Age.* Pink argues that there is a national craving for aesthetic appeal. Americans don't just want any toilet bowl brush, he argues. They want a *designer* toilet brush (hence the Michael Graves collection at Target). To remain at the forefront of the global economy, he argues, will require American workers to be the creative forces, the visionaries, the team players who work together to create aesthetically outstanding ideas.

Think back to *Champions of Change,* which contains a summary of research by Judith Burton and her team from Columbia University, who found that students in schools with rich arts programs scored higher than other students in taking risks, thinking imaginatively and creatively, and working cooperatively. Their survey of teachers in these schools revealed that learning through the arts developed children in five areas:

- the ability to share ideas openly;
- the ability to relate information while working through a complex problem;
- the ability to see a situation from multiple points of view while working toward a solution;
- the ability to synthesize ideas into a meaningful product; and
- the ability to sustain focus.

As this research shows, the arts clearly prepare the kinds of flexible thinkers and workers that futurists believe America needs in the next generation. Our challenge is to share the power of the arts with students and decision makers.

■ CONCLUSION

How do we prepare students to be the creative thinkers of the global economy? By engaging them creatively in their learning. By challenging them with open-ended team activities that reach far beyond standardized tests. By providing forums to practice public speaking and putting forth a cogent set of ideas. By giving them scaffolded learning activities that engage the mind and delight the imagination. That's what this book is all about.

■ REFERENCES

Americans for the Arts. n.d. Highlights from Key National Research on Arts Education. Available at http://www. americansforthearts.org/public_awareness/articles/002.asp (accessed January 13, 2007).

Deasy, Richard J., ed. 2002. *Critical Links: Learning in the Arts and Social and Academic and Social Development.* Arts Education Partnership. Available at http://www.aep-arts.org/publications (accessed January 13, 2007).

Fiske, Edward B., ed. 1999. *Champions of Change: The Impact of the Arts on Learning.* Arts Education Partnership and the President's Committee on Arts and Humanities. Available at http://www.aep-arts.org/publications (accessed January 13, 2007).

Friedman, Thomas J. 2005. *The World Is Flat.* 1st ed. New York: Farrar, Straus & Giroux. 488pp. ISBN 0374292884.

National Governors' Association. 2002. *The Impact of Arts Education on Workforce Preparation.* Available at http://www.nga.org/Files/pdf/050102ARTSED.pdf (accessed January 13, 2007).

Pink, Daniel H. 2005. *A Whole New Mind: Moving from the Information Age to the Conceptual Age.* New York: Riverhead Books. 260pp. ISBN 1573223085.

Chapter 2

Getting Started: Welcoming Rituals and Actors' Warm-ups (All Grades)

■ INTRODUCTION

One way to ensure that the arts are being used as an instructional method is to incorporate drama skill development into the lesson plan. Placing a Welcoming Ritual and warm-up activities at the start of each class period gives students regular practice developing their vocal and physical techniques, their imagination, and the self-discipline and self-control that are the hidden "backbone" essential for a drama project to succeed.

While these opening activities are important for students to grow as performers and learners, they have benefits for instructors as well. First, they are the instructor's first opportunity to set a positive, assertive classroom tone. Welcoming Rituals remind students of the media specialist's expectations while they are in the media center. But second, and perhaps more important, these activities give instructors the opportunity to make an initial assessment of their class. How students react to these brief activities demonstrates their current level of focus, gives a glimpse of how much stimulation and new challenge they are ready to take on, and provides insight into which students may need particular instructional attention, either because they are very reserved or very boisterous in their participation level.

■ WELCOMING RITUALS

A Welcoming Ritual is any activity that opens a class period, greets students, and reminds them of the expectations of the class. Many media specialists already incorporate Welcoming Rituals into their class: a repeated poem or song that begins each class visit. The term "Welcoming Ritual" is adapted from the term "Actor's Ritual," developed by Sean Layne (2002).

The word *ritual* is used deliberately here. A ritual is a highly structured, repetitive, yet meaningful activity. When selecting a Welcoming Ritual, choose one that can be repeated, perhaps for years, as rituals should become automatic processes for students. In this way, rituals are reassuring to students: they feel comfort and security knowing that the class begins in a predictable way.

A Welcoming Ritual can communicate many different ideas, including

- classroom expectations, such as respect for each other, listening, taking turns, or sharing;
- a preview of the activity of the day; and
- expected skills students will use that day.

Welcoming Rituals can be a chant or a song or a rhyme. They work best when reinforced with a physical set of gestures or movements. This is particularly effective for restless students, as it gives them permission to *move appropriately* in the media center.

Regardless of the type of ritual chosen, begin by arranging the students in a circle or square. An enclosed shape draws the class together into a cohesive unit. Each child is turned inward toward the others, creating a safe, enclosed space. With students in a circle, I am able to see all students at once.

My library has a big circle of contrasting carpet, and so I refer to this area throughout the book as the "circle area." Students gather around the perimeter of the circle. However, it is just as easy to create a playing space in a square or rectangular shape, depending on the available space. A 12-by-12-foot space is ideal. Students should be able to stand rather close together, but there should be room for everyone—including the instructors—in the circle. To create a circle or square, place thin strips of carpet tape in a contrasting color (ask the custodian first, as the tape sometimes leaves residue, even if the label promises it will not). Alternatively, define the space by laying down Velcro™ strips with the sticky "hook" side down on the carpet—the gripping action holds to the carpet without residual damage. Velcro costs approximately $3.00/yard. Kelner and Flynn (2006) recommend blue painter's tape but discourage the use of masking tape, as it is difficult to pull up. Avoid laying down an extra layer of carpet, as students could trip over the edges during kinesthetic activities.

A marked circle or square area helps students quickly assemble, just as carpet squares can be used to quickly identify the space where children will sit to hear a story. This area will also help define the playing space for activities in future chapters.

Begin each class by gathering in this circle, even if the day's lesson does not have a drama focus. It is valuable for centering, focusing, and settling young bodies and minds and preparing them for learning.

Begin by taking a few collective deep breaths. After traveling through the hallways, this release is often therapeutic for students. And for media specialists, who are often frantically running from the computer lab or the stacks just in time for class, it helps to become centered and focused as well. The work of Becky Bailey's *Conscious Discipline* (www.lovingguidance.com) also affirms the value of deep breathing for relieving stress and refocusing the young child.

Deep Breaths

Say, "Breathe in through your nose, and out through your mouth." A gentle, audible exhalation is fine, but if the breath is an exaggerated "huff," repeat the request. Clarify the instructions by saying, "This time, take a very gentle breath." There is no need to reprimand children if they don't do this gently the first time. This simple reminder—plus the repetition of the deep breath—is usually enough to correct students who are just being silly. A useful metaphor is to ask students to envision a birthday cake with lit candles. Ask them to breathe so gently that the candles will not go out. Repeat the breath a few times until the class feels relaxed and ready.

This is a great tool throughout the lesson. Return to, "Breathe in through your nose and out through your mouth" if the class loses focus or becomes overly talkative during the lesson. The mere act of breathing precludes students from talking just for a moment, and that is usually long enough to refocus the students' attention on the lesson. Often, it is as effective as, "Be good listeners!" or, "Let's stop talking now!"—with the benefit that the breath is soothing to the instructor and the student, whereas words sometimes betray frustration or anxiety. These few seconds provide a chance to become centered and calm for the lesson.

Following these deep breaths should come one of the following Welcoming Rituals. Each Welcoming Ritual focuses on the same skills. Many teaching artists have identified a core set of skills for drama work. For example, Oreck (2006) identifies physical awareness, collaboration, focus/commitment, and imagination as drama's key areas. Kelner and Flynn (2006) identify three acting tools—imagination/mind, voice, and body—and two acting skills, cooperation and concentration. Layne (2002) introduces the tools as voice, body, and imagination and echoes Kelner and Flynn's two acting skills. With elementary students, I have found Layne's list—body, voice, imagination, concentration, and cooperation—to be the most useful, and it is these five points that will be present in each Welcoming Ritual.

Welcoming Ritual 1: A Song—"When We're in the Media Center"

One way to begin, especially with early childhood students, is with a song. This song should be used at each class period as part of the overall structure of a student's visit to the media center, regardless of whether the lesson is performance centered.

Customized Welcoming Ritual songs can be created by setting new words to common public domain folk tunes.

This ritual is set to the tune of "Here We Go 'Round the Mulberry Bush." Notice how hand gestures reinforce the ideas and keep busy young bodies active. Especially with young children, it is important to scatter kinesthetic and physical activities throughout the lesson, as few early elementary students can sustain quiet stillness for 30 minutes or so.

Lyric	Physical Movement
Verse 1. When we're in the media center, media center, media center.	Walk clockwise around the perimeter of the circle to the beat of the music.
When we're in the media center, we all work together.	Place arms around the shoulders of the people on both sides.
Verse 2. When we're in the media center, media center, media center.	Walk clockwise around the perimeter of the circle to the beat of the music.
When we're in the media center, we use imagination.	Swirl both hands above the head to show "imagination."
Verse 3. When we're in the media center, media center, media center.	Walk clockwise around the perimeter of the circle to the beat of the music.
When we're in the media center, we practice self-control.	Make hands into fists; pose body-builder style to show how "strong" one's self-control is.

▶ Verse to Add When Doing Drama Work

Verse 4. When we act in the media center, media center, media center.	Hold arms out in front. Then gesture them outward three times as if showing off to an invisible audience.
When we act in the media center, we use our bodies and voices.	For "bodies," put hands on hips. For "voices," put hands to lips, then draw them away (like the charades gesture for "song").

A shorter option can be sung to the tune of, "Row, Row, Row Your Boat":

>Bodies, voices, imagination
>Are the tools we use,
>Concentration and cooperation
>Are the habits we choose.

Songs act as mnemonic devices, making them more easily memorized and recalled by students.

Welcoming Ritual 2: A Rhyme or Chant

Another effective Welcoming Ritual involves a favorite rhyme, poem, or chant. A chant is a spoken word activity in which all members of the class recite the same words at the same time. When explaining this version to the students, you might say it's like the Pledge of Allegiance, which everyone says at the same time. But in the media center, the chants should have more energy and enthusiasm.

Like the other ritual options, a chant is a series of phrases accompanied by body movements. It reminds students of the basic guidelines of the class. Teachers may have different behavioral expectations for students, but these phrases are general enough to coalesce with most rules.

When teaching a chant, it might be useful to teach a part of the text at a time, adding a few lines with each subsequent visit until the students have memorized the entire chant. This helps particularly if there is a high degree of absenteeism; students who are absent have an opportunity to catch up. Until the text is mastered, review the chant at the end of the media class when the children are lined up and waiting to leave.

This sample chant is told in limerick form, appealing to children because of its sing-song rhythm and rhyme.

▶ *General Chant*

Words of the Chant	Physical Movement
We come every week for a stay	March in place.
To learn and to grow in new ways	Tap forehead with index finger.
We all help out	Place arms around the shoulders of the students on both sides.
We don't run or shout	Wag finger in a "don't do it" gesture.
We find something new every day.	Hand up to forehead; look around (as if a sailor looking out to sea and covering his forehead to protect his eyes from the sun).

▶ *Verse to Add When Doing Drama Work*

Words of the Chant	Physical Movement
Today is a quite special day.	Cross arms and clutch hands at chest.
We're going to put on a play!	Pose with one foot in front of the other in one's *most* Shakespearean pose.
To make our creation	Tap finger on temple to show "thinking."
We'll need imagination	Swirl hands above head to show "imagination."
And our bodies and voices today!	For "bodies," place hands on hips. For "voices," put hands to lips, then draw them away (like the charades gesture for "song").

Kelner and Flynn (2006) recommend simply restating the five areas—body, voice, imagination, concentration, and cooperation—as a faster chanting option that is better suited to older students.

Video Resources for Welcoming Rituals

For more ideas for Welcoming Rituals, the following video resources may be useful.

Teaching artist Sean Layne uses the term "Actor's Ritual" instead of "Welcoming Ritual." In the 2002 Kennedy Center video demonstrating theatrical techniques, he models how a review of acting tools and skills has a positive impact on students' main lesson drama work. The video *Living Pictures: A Theatrical Technique for Learning Across the Curriculum* shows several warm-up activities and the drama technique of tableau, which we explore later in this book. It can be purchased from the Kennedy Center at http://www.kennedy-center.org/education/pdot/livingpictures/.

Subscribers to UnitedStreaming, the digital video service, may type "tableau" into the search box to find the video called *Teacher to Teacher: Professional Development for Today's Classroom: Language Arts Volume II* and view the section called "Integrating Drama into Language Arts and Social Studies" to see how Melanie Rick, a Virginia elementary teacher, has used Sean Layne's "Actor's Ritual" to prepare her students for drama work. She uses the ritual to ask students to commit to the upcoming drama work.

When Students Disrupt or Do Not Participate in the Welcoming Ritual

What if children do not participate or are disruptive? This is a legitimate concern and one that may crop up during any of the creative lessons discussed in this book.

Many children are not accustomed to working with quiet and sustained movements, and a few children may become restless or act out the first few times the ritual is performed.

Sometimes, this happens just because sustained drama work is an activity that is unfortunately foreign to many schools. "Sing in the library? Chant in the media center? When the *old librarian* was here, she never made us do that. She just let us sit down."

Remember—the Welcoming Ritual has value, or you would not dedicate precious instructional time to it. It is important that students respect the ritual. Sometimes there are students who are not in strong control of their kinesthetic or vocal selves on a given day. Do not allow their disruptions to affect the class.

If the class is interrupted by a student's outburst or by a student who is mocking the process, simply say, "I'm sorry. We need to start over again," and the entire Welcoming Ritual begins again. Disruptive students who dislike the controlled atmosphere of the Welcoming Ritual certainly don't like to experience it over and over, and they quickly join the group.

These opening activities take no more than two minutes, but they do so much to set the stage (so to speak) for a successful class. Once the opening routines are concluded, students are ready to begin warming up the "tools" mentioned in the rituals.

■ THE IMPORTANCE OF WARM-UP ACTIVITIES

The warm-up activities here are divided into two categories: vocal warm-ups and warm-up games. The primary focus of vocal warm-ups is to prepare the voice and imagination for drama work. The primary focus of warm-up games is to prepare the body for kinesthetic movement.

Whereas the Welcoming Ritual is controlled and structured, warm-up games have a more whimsical and playful atmosphere. They help to "warm up" students' acting skills and help them concentrate and work together. The best side benefit to warm-up activities is that children often don't realize these skills are being built, because they are perceived as so much fun!

Warm-ups are not optional; they are essential ingredients for a successful lesson. Our colleagues in physical education have known this for years—students do not enter the gym and immediately run a mile. They begin with stretches, making their bodies ready for the larger task. The stretching exercises aren't "optional"—they are there to prepare the athletes. These activities do the same thing.

Similarly, warm-ups are not stand-alone activities. They should be used in preparation for a main lesson and, after the first time they are introduced to students, can comprise as little as five minutes of a lesson.

When considering appropriate warm-up activities, make sure there is a correlation between the benefits of the activity and the forthcoming main lesson. Warm-ups should help children "practice" a drama skill that will be needed again in the main lesson. In general, a strong warm-up activity should fulfill at least one of these criteria:

> • Building physical flexibility so that the student is ready to move
>
> • Warming up the voice and preparing it to be used creatively
>
> • Igniting creative imagination and problem solving
>
> • Strengthening teamwork and students' ability to work in a group
>
> • Helping students focus their energy and self-control

Later chapters that discuss main lessons that integrate drama refer back to these warm-up activities. With practice, preferred warm-up activities will emerge to prepare students best for selected projects. When strong warm-up choices are made, they remain interesting and useful for students.

Great warm-up activities exist in drama, but many of the games played at camp or in scouting activities are also good options. The following are several examples of warm-up activities. Each discussion points out the key skills that will be exercised, as well as the grade levels that will benefit most from the activities.

■Vocal Warm-ups

This category of warm-ups concentrates on the voice. They can be done while standing on the Welcoming Ritual circle, while walking around the room, or while seated.

Tongue Twisters: To Build Vocal Articulation and Speed (All Ages)

To *articulate* is to move parts of the mouth and jaw so that one's speech can be heard accurately. To be able to share text with an audience, students must be able to speak in a way that the words are understood. This requires exercising those muscles by *overarticulation* of the lips, teeth, and tongue (Kelner and Flynn 2006). Overarticulation is an exaggeration of facial parts to make a more deliberate sound.

Imagine that you are speaking to someone who has a hearing impairment and relies on lip-reading. Say out loud the words, "Our tee time for golf is at seven," while looking in the mirror. Notice how, when speaking to someone with limited hearing ability, we naturally stretch our lips outward, up, out, or in, depending on the sound. The tongue pushes against the upper-front palate for "tee" and "time," and the teeth and jaw draw closed.

Professional stage actors are concerned about articulation because their voices must reach the back of a theatre. To practice articulation, they overarticulate and exaggerate their muscles.

Tongue twisters are the actor's most common articulation exercise. Try a handful of these with the students. Start slowly, focusing on a clear delivery of the sounds. Repeat, slowly accelerating in speed. Gain speed only to the point where the articulation remains clear. When clarity is sacrificed for speed, slow down. The goal of this exercise is not to see who finishes first!

- School shoes, beach shoes.
- Shakespeare sure should sugar some shallots.
- Madge met Matt and made macaroons.
- Quinton quickly quitted the quiz.
- The right light is a night light, not a bright light.
- Dewey does dozens of decimals all day.

Extension. For more tongue twisters, try the Tongue Twister database at http://www.geocities.com/athens/8136/tonguetwisters.html or engage students in writing their own using Leslie Opp-Beckman's tongue twister lesson at http://darkwing.uoregon.edu/~leslieob/twisters.html.

I Like to Eat: To Develop Vocal Articulation (All Ages)

A classic camp game is to chant, "I like to eat, I like to eat, I like to eat, eat apples and bananas." With each verse, a single vowel is substituted for all vowels in the sentence, creating silly nonsense sounds. Imagine the stereotype of the snooty, wealthy dowager, nose turned up, with impeccable articulation. Say,

---

Oh, class, today I would like to share a very special secret with you. And then I would like you to repeat it after me:

I like to eat, I like to eat, I like to eat, eat apples and bananas.

(*Students repeat.*)

Very good. Let's do it together this time, only this time, let's use only the long "A" vowel sound:

A lake tay ate, A lake tay ate, A lake tay ate, ate ay-pls ay-nd bay-nay-nays.

Wait a minute. That sounds odd. Let's try it again using only the long "E" sound:

Eee leek tee eat, Eee leek tee eat, Eee leek tee eat, eat eeples eend bee-nee-nees.

Hmm. How about with the long "I" sound? And this time, let's really articulate!

I like tie ite, I like tie ite, I like tie ite, ite eye-ples eye-nd by-ny-nys.

How about the long "O" sound?

Oh loke toe oat, Oh loke toe oat, Oh loke toe oat, ote opals ond boe-noe-noes.

Let's end with the long "U" sound.

You luke too oot, You luke too oot, You luke too oot, oot ooples oond bu-nu-nus!

These nonsensical sentences stretch and exercise vocal muscles, building strength and articulation.

How Would You Say It?: To Develop Vocal Variety (All Ages)

Vocal variety is a general term for manipulating the voice to change how it sounds. Think of a great storyteller. What made the performance so outstanding? The text of the story, sure, and the dramatic way he or she moved. But something else makes a storyteller truly outstanding: the way he or she manipulates his or her voice. Children telling ghost stories during sleepovers know of the power of vocal variety—how the voice slows down, quiets, and gets a lower pitch just before the scariest part, how the voice speeds up and gets higher as the victims run away from the ghost.

Vocal variety is an important skill for developing and sharing the personality of a stage character. The voice can be changed in many ways, including the following:

- **Pitch.** Pitch is determined by the register of the voice—low or high. For example, *Sesame Street's* Elmo has a high-pitched voice, while the same show's Snuffleupagus and Disney's Eeyore have low, resonant voices. In music, sopranos have high-pitched voices, and basses have low-pitched voices. Pitch can help establish character: high-pitched voices are often considered to be childlike or happy, while low-pitched voices can be perceived as adult, all-knowing, somber, or sad.

- **Speed.** Speed refers to how fast or slow a person is talking. Characters who speak quickly can be perceived as excited, frightened, or nervous. Characters who speak slowly can be considered dull, bored, listless, or uninteresting.

- **Volume.** Volume refers to loudness or softness. A certain amount of volume is required in order for an audience to hear an actor's text. Loud voices can be perceived as strong, confident, bossy, or in-charge. Soft voices can be affiliated with small animals, shy children, or plotting thieves.

- **Tone/Energy.** Energy is affiliated with emotion and emphasis. It is the extra "oomph" that carries meaning into the voice. Emotions like happiness, sadness, loneliness, or fear can be expressed through the voice.

This exercise calls on students to practice these skills. Print out a copy of the form on page 19, which features a series of short sentences, onto an overhead transparency. Cut along the dotted lines and place the contents in a small coffee can or box labeled "sentences." This form has a series of short, neutral sentences. Repeat with the form on page 20, which contains a series of vocal variety prompts, and place the pieces in a container labeled "vocal variety."

Sentences for *How Would You Say It?*

I lost my homework.	You have gum in your hair.
I found a cat.	I lost it.
Where is my wallet?	I found it.
What time is it?	I won.
Nice to meet you.	I lost.
I won the lottery.	I love it.
I got an A.	I hate it.
I failed the test.	Excuse me.
My basketball is on the roof.	There's a bear.
You're on fire!	I'm sorry.

Prompts for *How Would You Say It?*

Say it LOUDLY.	Say it with a SCARED voice.
Say it SOFTLY.	Say it with a BRAVE voice.
Say it with a HIGH VOICE.	Say it in a CONFIDENT voice.
Say it with a LOW voice.	Say it in an UNSURE voice.
Say it SLOWLY.	Say it QUIETLY.
Say it QUICKLY.	Say it like it's a SECRET.
Say it like you're ANGRY.	Say it like you're SAD.
Say it like you're HAPPY.	Say it like a PRINCIPAL.
Say it like you're EXCITED.	Say it like a ROCK STAR.
Say it like you're OUT OF BREATH.	Yell it ACROSS THE STREET.

Ask for a volunteer to pull a sentence from each container and place the two pieces on the overhead. Say,

On the count of three, say this sentence (*point to it*) with this technique (*point to the other piece*). Ready? One-two-three.

Repeat a few times.

Extension. Draw one slip from the sentence container and two or more from the vocal variety canister.

"Tall, Small, Wide, Skinny": To Develop Flexible Bodies and Voices (Grades K–2)

When working with students, it can be surprising to discover that the same students whose body movements are spontaneous and energetic as they walk into the media center become staid and shy when a drama activity commences. (Think back to student productions at which the kids just seemed to *stand* there, as if someone had fixed the soles of their shoes to the ground.)

"Tall, Small, Wide, Skinny" is a valuable warm-up for nurturing a more flexible range of motion and to develop a shorthand vocabulary for use during main lesson drama work.

Invite students to stand in a circle. Say, "Repeat after me." Raise the arms high above the head and stand on tiptoe, calling "tall" in a confident, assertive voice.

Then crouch down low on the ground, covering the head with the hands and say, in a high-pitched voice, "small." If children respond minimally, say, "Can you get even smaller? Can you be as small as an egg? As small as an acorn?" to encourage them to shrink themselves even further.

Then stand with the feet as wide apart as possible, arms open wide, and say in a honeyed voice, "wide." Finally, stand stiffly at attention, legs firmly pressed together, arms flattened at the sides. In a high-pitched, pinched voice, call, "skinny."

When I work with early elementary students, we do several stories in which students must quickly contort their bodies into the shape of the growing plant or of different animals. Being able to call out, "Can you make your peacock with a wide body?" or to say, "The seeds begin with a small body and then grow up and up and up until they are tall" has proven to be an effective and fast way to nudge students into more expressive and committed body shapes.

Modification: Students with limited body control may bump into each other when creating "wide." If this occurs, consider spreading out the students in a large, open space. Have them hold their arms out and gently rotate them to make sure they won't touch any other student.

Extension: Adding the voice. This activity also builds strong voices. When calling "tall," use a deep, loud voice and ask students to say it back as they make the gesture. "Small" gets a tiny, high-pitched voice. Speak "wide" with a wide smile and a honeyed voice, and "skinny" with a tight, nasal voice and pursed lips.

The "Drum Game": To Build Body Control and Concentration (Best with Grades K–2)

In his workshops, Sean Layne often points out that educators do not instruct children on how to concentrate, yet we expect young children to concentrate upon request. Imagine if we did this with math. On the first day of first grade, the teachers would say, "OK. Time to add!" and leave out instruction. That would be a disaster. Of course classroom teachers are expected to give scaffolded instruction in math, just as drama leaders must give practice time to concentration.

The "Drum Game"—an activity common with many drama practitioners and recorded in many manuals—helps students practice body and voice control. The game is simple to play and effectively hones children's focus, concentration, and responsiveness to instruction.

To begin, select a small, handheld drum. One with a quiet, pleasant sound is preferable. A good option is the plastic case that comes with a spool of CDs, with a fat marker for a drumstick. Students will naturally remain quieter and focused if they have to strain a bit to hear the sound. If a loud, brassy drum is used, students may murmur or chat quietly during the game, defeating the concentration-building value of the exercise.

Next, define the playing space, the part of the room to which the activity should be confined. With small children, the "Drum Game" may be played within the taped area used for the Welcoming Ritual.

Say to the students,

> We are going to play the "Drum Game." I will play this drum (*demonstrate*). When you hear the drum beat, you walk to the beat of the music. But when the drum stops, you stop. This is a game with no talking and no touching. Ready? Go.

Experiment with playing the drum for a few beats, then stopping. Try varying the rhythm and speed of the drum. This is another opportunity to watch students and gain assessment of their conduct. Which children use their bodies in creative and interesting ways? Which are having difficulty controlling themselves? Which two children seem to be playing together and may not make good project partners later on? Which children are working very hard to succeed? Is there a child who doesn't seem defiant but is having difficulty processing the stimuli?

Play this game without penalty for the first few classes. As discussed before, some children do push the boundaries of the game. Some are simply easily distracted and may absentmindedly wander off and begin looking at books or chatting. A small number may behave mischievously toward others. These behaviors are a sign that the students do not have control over their bodies and that concentration is weak.

If you notice this, implement a new rule. Say,

> This time, if you talk, I'll ask you to leave the game and wait here (*demonstrate*). If you touch someone or something, I'll ask you to step out of the game.

Make sure to follow through so that students respect boundaries. Resist the urge to overlook a star pupil's chatter; it is important to follow through with the rules. This does not have to be traumatic for children; a child only needs to be out for a few rounds, not for the remainder of the activity. This is plenty of time for students to observe others' conduct and resolve to make a better choice. After a few rounds of being "out," quietly check with the student: "Do you know why you were out?" He or she should be able to answer accurately, and if so, ask if he or she will do it again if allowed to go back into the game. If the student says no, invite him or her back into the game. If a student is unable to articulate why he or she was out or how to change his or her behavior, gently remind the student, then play a few more rounds before asking again. It is important to connect students' participation with their understanding of the impact of their behavioral choices.

Other terms for stepping out or leaving the game include popularly accepted athletic phrases, like "wait on the sidelines" or "sit on the bench," or theatrical metaphors, like "Please wait backstage" or "Please wait in the wings."

Extension: Body shapes. While kindergarteners and first graders can repeat this activity for the entire year without getting bored, you may wish to make the activity more complex or vary it to maintain the interest of older students. During the game, call out different body shapes, such as "tall," "small," "wide," or "skinny." Ask them to move to the drum beat with their bodies in that position.

Extension: Levels. Dancers are particularly interested in "levels"—that is, how high the body is positioned relative to the ground. Students can be encouraged to play this game with low, medium, or high levels. Demonstrate this with the following examples:

- *Low level:* Crawling, crouching, keeping the entire body lower than waist level.

- *Medium level:* Basic walking, either with arms to the side or stretched out. Nothing in the body is raised above the head.

- *High level:* Tiptoeing, reaching, high flying.

Extension: Energy. "Energy" is another term used by dancers to describe kinesthetic movement. Ask students to move to the beat of the drum. Call out a variety of words. They should continue to listen to the drum but should also incorporate the word called into their movement. Some useful words and possible student movements are listed below. Try not to model possible movements for students; let them explore this for themselves. A much richer and more varied set of responses will emerge. If students have strong musical vocabulary (check with the building's music teacher), try the music terms explored below.

- *Angry* or *sharp* or *staccato.* Movements might include sharp, angular motions, heavy footsteps or stomping, or sharp hand thrusts.

- *Floating* or *legato.* Movements might appear gentle, flowing, or loose.

- *Happy* or *cheerful.* Movements might include bouncing steps or smiles. Very expressive children might leap or jump.

> • *Scared* or *frightened* or *nervous.* The students may contract their bodies, tiptoe, sneak, or proceed cautiously.
>
> • *Running late* or *worried.* Movements appear hurried; the body tends to be tighter and less expressive. Students may consult real or imaginary clocks or watches. The face may look anxious.

Extension: Recorded music. This game also works with recorded music in lieu of the drum. To use recorded music, find a few examples of music with varying rhythms, speeds, and styles. A good all-in-one-CD source for this is Gustav Holst's *The Planets,* a musical composition with a separate movement for each of eight planets. Randomly select a track and allow it to run for 10 to 15 seconds. Encourage students to move at the same pace as the beat of the music but also to try to interpret the music with their bodies. For example, Holst's "Mars" movement is brash and military. Students might march like soldiers, salute, or prepare for battle. "Neptune," on the other hand, is mystical and might encourage floating, smooth gestures. If students have difficulty coming up with different body movements, call out suggestions to them.

Extension: Lead the way! To build further physical flexibility that can lead to a stronger physicality during drama work, play the game and call out different body parts that will "lead" them across the room. If "Lead with your nose," is called out, students should walk as if someone has tied a rope through their noses and they are walking nose first. Calling, "Lead with your stomach" should cause students to walk with bloated stomachs in front and the rest of their bodies leaning back. "Lead with your ear" would cause students to walk somewhat sideways, their ears in the front of their bodies. I learned this exercise while attending the Royal Shakespeare Company's Prince of Wales Shakespeare School. This exercise requires students to move their bodies in new and unexpected ways, loosening body rigidity and exploring alternate methods of ambulation that students can call on later when developing characters.

"Stop, Go, Jump, Clap": To Strengthen Body Control, Listening, and Concentration (Grades K–12)

This game comes from Mary Johnson, a drama educator with the Royal Shakespeare Company. It does wonders for building body control and developing listening skills. It works well with students of all ages.

Like the "Drum Game," this activity is done in a large, open space. Explain that this game has four commands that will be called out by the leader. Say,

> In this game, you will walk around the room. I will call out four actions that I want you to take. When I say Stop, you Stop. When I say Go, you walk around the room. When I say Jump, you jump one time. When I say Clap, you clap one time. There is no talking or touching. Ready, Set, Go!

This portion of the exercise is very literal and simply asks students to follow directions. The fun comes when the class progresses to round two. Say,

> Not bad. Looks like you're ready for this game to get a little bit harder. Now let's play Backward Style. This time, when I stay Stop, you go. When I say Go, you stop. When I say Jump, you clap. When I say Clap, you jump. Ready, Set, Go!

There is usually an initial lurch of movement before students remember that in this round, "Go" means "Stop"!

It may appear that this activity is too difficult to be used with kindergarteners or students with special needs, but both populations respond enthusiastically. After just a few weeks of trying this game, kindergarten students are as expert as older children. In fact, students tend to be stronger players at this game than adults—perhaps it is adults' years of following directions that makes it so tricky for them to adapt.

Johnson believes this activity stimulates the students' creative right brain, which helps them think more creatively during the main drama lesson.

Revision: Bundling commands. For older students, an additional challenge can be to cluster two or three movements into a single command. For example, the instructor might say, "stop-clap-jump," and the students would perform all three actions in rapid succession. Bundling commands when playing the game "backwards" can cause anxiety in some high-achieving students. Watch students carefully to be sure the game remains fun and effective.

"Mirrors": To Build Teamwork and Concentration (Grades K–12)

"Mirrors" is another classic dramatic warm-up that has been used by countless drama practitioners and writers. Ask students to choose a partner (the instructor can also pair up students, but that tends to take longer than the activity itself). Ask them to name one student "A" and the other "B." The game begins with Person A acting as the mirror for Person B. Person B begins by moving his or her body slowly and deliberately, stretching out tall or wide, standing or kneeling or squatting, and A must try to mimic B's every move. After a few minutes, switch roles. B is now the mirror, and A initiates the activity.

When I learned this game as a child, I remember seeing some students who tried to move jerkily or quickly to try to catch their partners off-guard. Trying to get a partner to goof up is not the goal of this activity. I heard a wonderful explanation of the goal of this exercise in fall 2005, when I sat in on a student workshop led by members of the Handspring Puppet Company of South Africa. One of the company's members pointed out an important distinction: the goal of "Mirrors" is to empower one's partner to successfully mimic one's actions, to move in synchronicity with the partner. "Mirrors" is meant to encourage harmonious movement, not to create a competition between partners. The activity is about *success,* not about trying to outsmart the mirror.

The level of concentration and teamwork during this activity is astounding. Although early elementary students cannot sustain this activity for more than a minute or two per round, it is still a worthy activity for focusing and centering attention. This activity is feasible for kindergarteners if the rounds are kept short.

"Make Me a . . . ": To Strengthen Teamwork, Collaboration, Imagination, Physical Expression, and Working Efficiently (Grades K–12)

This is another activity that is common in the theatrical community. Johnson and Layne are two of the practitioners of this technique. The activity asks students to use their bodies to create physical objects and to use their bodies to represent thematic concepts. It can be played with each child working alone, but when expanded into a small group activity, it becomes a powerful exercise in creativity and teamwork.

If each child is working independently, spread the students out in an area that is at least 12 feet by 12 feet. Remind them of any boundaries (e.g., "Stay in the open space, away from the shelves.").

Then explain the game rules. Say,

> Each student will use his or her body to portray the object or theme given in the time frame announced. For example, "By the time I count to ten, make me a _____. When we get to ten, freeze into place and we'll look at what everyone made. Some of the things I'm calling out will be objects, and you'll be able to make your body look just like the object. But as the game goes on, there may be some things that I call out that are *ideas*. You'll really need to use your imagination to think of how to show me those things."

Possible objects or ideas include a flower, a tree, a chair, a table, and friendship.

When students freeze, give them a moment to look around the room (staying in position) to see the variety of interpretations. If many groups have similar interpretations, try saying, "Now you have until the count of 10 to make me a *different* version of a _____." This gets the right brain engaged in creative thinking.

Variation: Groups. Divide the class into groups of four or five students. The goal is to have enough students to create an interesting picture but not so many that it becomes difficult to negotiate a plan in limited time. Remind students that their goal is to work together; for example, if the instructions are to make a house, the goal is *one* house, not five houses, in a particular group. The groups must collaborate *without speaking*. If working with young children, it may be useful to brainstorm strategies for working without oral discussion. These strategies include hand signals, pointing, or modeling for a teammate. The discussion-free environment prevents arguments in which the loudest voice would dominate decision making. It heightens students' need to rely on each other and work interdependently.

In addition, limit the collaborative time to approximately one minute (or less if the instructor senses that students have completed the task ahead of schedule). Condensing the work time coerces students into making decisions quickly and precludes becoming quagmired in lengthy negotiations. Again, scaffold the list to move from the concrete to the abstract. Possible objects or ideas for this variation include a house,

a boat (this may be difficult for urban students),

a lawnmower (this may be difficult for urban students),

a skyscraper,

a washing machine,

joy,

love,

anger, and

fear.

Extension: Connection to the main lesson. Select concrete objects or thematic concepts from the story or research lesson that is to follow and call these out. For example, if the story of the day is Chris Van Allsburg's *The Polar Express,* the following might be suitable:

Sleeping

Santa

Bell

Sleigh

Train

Believing

Notice how the items are organized from most concrete (easiest) to most abstract (most difficult). This scaffolding is important. Students need the success of the easier tasks to bolster them in the more difficult challenges.

Tapping into students' prior knowledge is a common activity before introducing a new unit of content. "Make Me a . . . " can be used to activate students' existing knowledge. Create a list of objects and ideas related to the upcoming unit of study. For example, for "Pioneers," the list might include a covered wagon, a trail, and cooking over an open fire.

Extension: Transitions. Post a list of four or five topics where the entire class can see it. Once the class is divided into groups of three to five students, call out each topic one at a time. Then tell the students that they will string together the topics to make one "performance." You will give them five counts to transition their bodies—without talking—from their first pose to their second pose. The transition should have a theatrical feel rather than being merely a "get from Point A to Point B" feeling. Ask, "How can you move your bodies in an interesting way between the two positions?" Allow students to quietly discuss the most effective means of moving their bodies from position to position. Repeat this until there is a transition between each. Ask each group to "perform" for the other. Given the more complex level of this activity, allow approximately 20 minutes. Recommended for grades 4 and up.

Extension: Sequencing. For a main lesson activity, repeat the transitions extension above, but this time ask the groups to sequence each of the items on the list in an order that has meaning for them. Allow 20 to 25 minutes. Recommended for grades 5 and up.

Pantomime: To Strengthen Concentration, Focus, and Physical Expression (Grades K–12)

Pantomime refers to acting where there is no sound, only movement. No props are used. Therefore, movements must be specific, not vague, in order to communicate information. Pantomimes tell a story or demonstrate a process. There are several sources for pantomime topics.

Introduction of new vocabulary that will be used in the main lesson. Consult your research topic or read-aloud. Pantomime can be used to introduce new unit concepts or ideas. For example, it can be difficult for students studying the Gold Rush to understand the day-to-day labors of miners. Instructors can bring this experience to life by leading a pantomime activity in which they narrate the gold mining process while students create it with their bodies. When the pantomime is completed, ask students, "What did you learn about panning for gold from this activity?" Answers might include, "It's hard to crouch for that long," "They had to be really patient," or, "You'd want good shoes for this." All of these can better prepare students for the main lesson.

Classroom curriculum and content. If the goal of the pantomime warm-up is to help children practice more specific movements, then it may not be crucial to have a connection to the main lesson. Turn to the classroom teachers for suggestions. For example, when I taught in the all-kindergarten building, one of their fall instructional goals was to teach hand washing. At the same time, one of my fall goals was to help children become more physically expressive so they would be ready for meaningful drama work later in the year. I narrated pantomime (adding the voice) to mimic the hand-washing process, stepping up to the sink, cranking the paper towel dispenser, turning on the faucet, washing while we sang "Happy Birthday" to make sure they washed for long enough, turning off the water, ripping off the paper towel, drying hands, and disposing of the used towel.

Similarly, older students might pantomime the process of an upcoming science experiment or how to spin the combination lock to open their lockers.

Variation: Pass it on! Name an imaginary object and pantomime holding it. Then pass it around the circle, asking each student to handle "it" as if it were real. Examples of "objects" to use are

a baby rabbit or chick,

a hot bagel or potato,

a prickly porcupine,

a slippery pig,

a butterfly that has to be passed from cupped hand to cupped hand so it cannot fly away, and

a dirty facial tissue.

■ CONCLUSION

Drama warm-ups are important precursors to main lessons, strengthening the mental and physical "muscles" of students. The chapters that expand beyond warm-ups present a variety of main lessons in which children explore academic content and/or demonstrate their understanding.

■ REFERENCES

Discovery Channel School. 2005. *Teacher to Teacher: Professional Development for Today's Classroom: Language Arts Volume II.* Available at http://www.unitedstreaming.com/ (accessed January 15, 2007).

Kelner, Lenore Blank, and Rosalind Flynn. 2006. *A Dramatic Approach to Reading Comprehension.* Portsmouth, NH: Heinemann. 229pp. ISBN 0325007942.

Layne, Sean. 2001–2002. *Living Pictures: A Theatrical Technique for Learning Across the Curriculum.* Washington, DC: Kennedy Center. (VHS video). Available for purchase at http://www.kennedy-center.org/education/pdot/livingpictures.

Opp-Beckman, Leslie. 2004. *ESL PIZZAZ! Tongue Twisters.* Available at http://darkwing.uoregon.edu/~leslieob/twisters.html (accessed August 10, 2006).

Oreck, Barry. 2006. "Talent Assessment Process." *Teaching Artist Journal* 3(4): 220–227.

Spolin, Viola. 1999. *Improvisation for the Theater: A Handbook of Teaching and Directing Techniques.* 3d ed. Evanston, Ill: Northwestern University Press. 412pp. ISBN 081014008X.

Staley, C. T. 2003. *Tongue Twister Database.* Available at http://www.geocities.com/athens/8136/tonguetwisters.html (accessed August 10, 2006).

Chapter 3

Telling and Retelling Stories Through Drama: Narrative Pantomime and Circle Drama (Preschool and Up)

INTRODUCTION

This chapter and the next focus on drama as a tool to retell narratives. Kelner and Flynn (2006) refer to this type of activity as "story dramatization"; Sun (2003) refers to it as "dramatic story re-enactment." Retelling stories through drama calls on students to demonstrate two key skills. One is the ability to understand the elements of story: its plot, character, setting, and sequence of events. The second is the ability to demonstrate that understanding through dramatic action.

Pantomime is a method of performance in which participants act out events silently. Narrative pantomime is a variation of pantomime in which the participants act out events, without speaking, while the story is told or read aloud by a single narrator. One child or the media specialist acts as narrator; other participants use their bodies and facial expressions to demonstrate character and show the actions of the story. Children in the "audience" are called upon to provide sound effects. As students' skills develop, the story reenactment can expand beyond pantomime, as students add their voices through dialogue and teacher-initiated questions.

This chapter looks at two approaches to narrative pantomime. The first is the Storytime Model for preschool through third graders. In the Storytime Model, the instructor is the narrator, retelling a picture book, and the children act out the story. Circle drama is a variant of this technique that will also be discussed in this chapter.

The second model, the Creation Model, is for students in grades 4 and up, where the teacher steps out of the creative process and the students assume the responsibility for crafting new narratives based on knowledge gained during the research process.

Narrative pantomime is a wonderful introduction to drama for media specialists and students. Judy Freeman (2006) refers to it as a popular technique with students and media specialists alike. It focuses on improvisation instead of rehearsals, does not require its participants to be readers or to recall specific dialogue from the story, does not rely on memorization, and can be completed in the course of a single lesson.

Two metaphors may work well to explain the concept of narrative pantomime to children. One is to tell students to imagine that they are creating a television show—with the sound down all the way or the "mute" button pressed on the remote. Their bodies must communicate the meaning of the story because their voices will be silent. The instructor's job is to provide the voiceover. *Voiceover* is a film or television term that refers to a narrator's voice superimposed over the action of the story. The narrator is not seen; only the voice is heard. In narrative pantomime, the instructor-as-narrator stands to the side of the action but is not part of the stage picture.

Another way to explain narrative pantomime is to share *Officer Buckle and Gloria,* by Peggy Rathmann. In Rathmann's story, Officer Buckle's safety lectures become popular when he brings along his police dog, Gloria. Little does Officer Buckle realize that during his droning lectures, Gloria is silently and energetically acting out each safety tip behind his back. During their safety assemblies, Officer Buckle is the narrator, and Gloria performs the pantomime.

■ NARRATIVE PANTOMIME DURING STORYTIME, GRADES PRE-K–3

A successful narrative pantomime lesson has four steps. First, the class engages in the Welcoming Ritual, which focuses and settles children and reminds them of acting tools. Next, the students participate actively in storytime, looking for details that will later bring the story to life. Third, students warm up their bodies and voices. Finally—and only in the last few minutes of the class!—the students act in narrative pantomime.

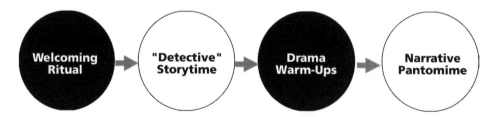

It is the combination of steps that makes narrative pantomime a meaningful activity, as the early steps prepare students for the later ones. Resist the urge to cut a step if time runs short, as a complete lesson can be completed in as few as 25 minutes or expanded to fill as many as 45 minutes. The process is especially effective for younger students, as it alternates kinesthetic with seated activities.

Step One: Welcoming Ritual

Chapter 2 discusses the importance and purpose of a Welcoming Ritual. Select one that works well with your student population.

Step Two: "Detective" Storytime

After the Welcoming Ritual, move to sharing the day's story. Media specialists have many unique approaches to storytime. Some teachers are able to share the story by asking the children to stay in their circle but to sit down. If telling the story from memory or with manipulatives or puppets, semicircle seating is a good choice. I sometimes want to tell a classic folktale in my own way that better prepares students for drama (by removing extra description and focusing on the dialogue and plot). When that is the case, the children sit in a circle. That way, I can create repeated phrases, streamline description, and focus on action without a child saying, "Hey! That's not the way it was in the book!" or, "Wait a minute! You're not reading the *real* words!"

Usually, however, I hold up the book for storytime. I sit in a chair in front of the students, who sit on the floor facing me. (I haven't had good luck displaying a book when the kids are sitting in a circle—I've had too many complaints from children who can't see.) The following diagram shows how my storytime area is arranged. Notice the empty space behind the students; this is used for the playing space during the narrative pantomime.

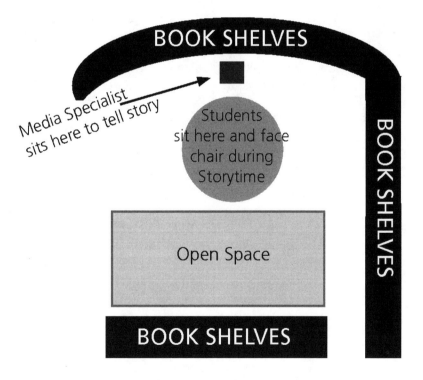

Sometimes it's important to reinforce the concept that stories are found in books. Using the book awakens children's visual learning. Drama is as visual as it is kinesthetic. Illustrations help to communicate inferences and details about characters, their world, and their behaviors that the text alone may not impart. Especially for nonreaders, "reading" illustrations is key to their understanding of books.

Often there are details in the illustrations that help the students create the dramatic elements later on. For example, I recently read Paul Galdone's classic adaptation of *The Three Billy Goats Gruff* to a kindergarten class. Students were so captivated by Galdone's repeated renderings of the meadow, daisies, and grass that they insisted that these scenic elements be featured in our production. These elements would not have been present had I told the story from memory or with dolls or puppets representing the characters.

Regardless of how the children are arranged, remind them to sit "body check style." "Body check style" means legs crossed, back straight, eyes on the person who is talking, and voices quiet. Once this has been defined a few times for students, say simply, "Body check yourselves," and everyone will straighten up. This is not merely a classroom management strategy; it is also useful during drama activities, as it keeps children's arms and legs away from the playing space.

Once the students are assembled, begin reading the story aloud. Make this as interactive an experience as possible. Ask students to predict what might happen next, based on what has already happened in the story. Ask students to demonstrate understanding.

Go beyond literary comprehension questions and get the body engaged as well. For example, say,

> Let's stop for a minute and look at this first illustration of Epossumondas (from Coleen Salley's *Why Epossumondas Has No Hair on His Tail*, illustrated by Janet Stevens). What can we learn about this character before the story even begins? What do we know about his age from the fact that he is wearing a diaper? What can we predict about the way Epossumondas might act during the story? What kind of body shape does he or she have? How do you think Epossumondas might walk? Let's walk around the story carpet as if we were Epossumondas. That's good! Now let's find out more about Epossumondas from the author and illustrator by reading the story.

Another metaphor for these storytime activities is to think of them as a production meeting. In theatre companies, a production meeting occurs when key players—the director, designers, stage managers, and staff—gather to plan the elements of the production and how those elements will work together to create a complete stage experience. As the story unfolds, discuss issues that will need to be expressed or resolved during the pantomime. In this way, the students' roles during storytime change from passive receivers to active interpreters of text. Empower students to think of themselves as "detectives," actively searching for details within text and illustrations that will bring their pantomimes to life.

This is also a time to develop memory aids for key phrases and actions in the story. Draw attention to phrases that are repeated throughout the story, encouraging students to speak them along with you. Later, during the pantomime, these will become choral speaking moments. *Choral speaking* means that a group is speaking the same text at the same time. While reading *Caps for Sale,* for example, the class might practice saying, "You monkeys, you! You give me back my caps!" Similarly, repeated actions can be created that will later engage students in the pantomime. For example, each time the story discusses the order of the caps stacked on the peddler's cap, students can mime stacking them higher and higher on top of their heads. These repetitions animate storytime and activate student learning.

It is also important to discuss safety issues with students. This is much more effective when done in advance instead of during the height of the drama. For example, in Jan Brett's *The Mitten,* a handful of animals fly out of the mitten when the bear sneezes. Pause during storytime to say, "When we act this out, how can we keep this moment safe?" Students can give their input, and a safe solution (such as agreeing to "fly" out of the mitten but go only as far as the tape line, where the students wait and watch the final scene quietly) can be agreed upon. The few moments it takes to gather student input and make a collaborative decision reap so many benefits. Just as a professional theatre company relies on trust, so does narrative pantomime. Students who are invested in what they are doing, who believe that their insight is meaningful to the group, take greater pride in their work. As a result, they cause fewer behavior problems.

Invest time during storytime in investigating and getting to know the story well. Pause for student questions. Save only 10 to 15 minutes in the lesson plan for the drama activity. The thinking and processing of the story happen now, during storytime.

Questions like these help stimulate children's abstract thinking and reinforce their understanding of the story. Asking students to physicalize actions helps in differentiating instruction. Those who cannot answer can look to their colleagues for a range of possibilities.

In addition, an interactive storytime taps into students' intrinsic motivation and excitement about what is to come.

Step Three: Warm-up Activities

Having sat still for the past several minutes, young learners will be eager to stand up and make their bodies active again. The next step in the process is to lead the class in a series of dramatic warm-ups.

These are essential to engage and prepare the five acting tools: body, voice, imagination, concentration, and cooperation. A good combination of warm-ups from chapter 2 includes the "Drum Game," "Stop, Go, Jump, Clap," "Tall, Small, Wide, Skinny," and "Make Me a . . .". Change games whenever you feel the class's energy is beginning to wane. About five minutes of warm-ups is plenty.

Step Four: Acting Out the Narrative Pantomime

Next, plan out the playing area for the narrative pantomime and transition the students into that space. "Playing area," "playing space," "acting stage," and "acting area" all define the physical space in which the acting will happen. In my media center, I have a large open space behind the storytime area. The children's backs are turned to this area during the story. To prepare for the drama, they simply turn 180 degrees to face the empty space. Where they are seated becomes the "audience." I step away from the chair and position myself just to the side of the children, angling my body so that I can see both the playing space and the "audience."

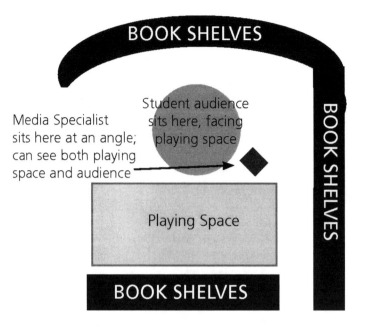

If space is limited, move the storytime chair out of the way to make room for the playing space or use the taped circle/square from chapter 2 as the boundary of the playing space.

The methods for acting out the story with narrative pantomime depend on the story that is chosen. With storytime pantomime, children can either perform "in unison" —that is, with each child performing the same action—or as a theatrical ensemble, with children performing different roles and other children making sound effects from the audience. The following sections explore these methods in detail.

■ NARRATIVE PANTOMIME IN UNISON FOR YOUNG CHILDREN (PRESCHOOL–GRADE 1)

Young children, from preschool through first grade, enjoy being "on stage" all the time. When all students are encouraged to perform the actions simultaneously, each child can fully engage without fear that he or she is "being watched" or "all alone on the stage."

Choosing a Book for Unison Pantomime

When selecting a book for unison pantomime, look for books that

- have a single lead protagonist or only one character at a time (characters can be human, animal, or even objects!);
- focus on action, not inner thoughts;
- can be completed without physical objects (props can be pantomimed); and
- last no more than 10 minutes to hold young students' interest.

A list of books suitable to narrative pantomime is included at the end of this section.

Ground Rules

Before your students stand up to begin the unison pantomime, review the ground rules. Because unison pantomime is best with very young students, limit the rules to just a few.

1. The teacher's job is to use her voice to tell the story.
2. The students' job is to use their bodies without talking to show what is happening in the story.
3. The students should stay in the storytime area during the activity.
4. Students who cannot control their bodies or voices may be asked to sit in chairs lined up at the back of the room.
5. Keep your hands to yourself. Do not touch another student unless the teacher asks you to.

Sample Unison Pantomime Lesson

To demonstrate unison pantomime, the classic Ruth Krauss/Crockett Johnson picture book, *The Carrot Seed,* is used. In this story, a little boy plants a seed and cares for it faithfully, even though his family claims that the seed won't grow. At the end of the story, a carrot does indeed grow.

The media specialist says,

You did a great job sharing that story with me. Now we're going to pretend that we are inside the story. Who remembers who the most important person in the story was? . . . That's right, the boy who planted the seed . And who tells him that the seed won't grow? . . . Yes, his family. And what important thing happens at the end? . . . You're right. The seed grows. We are going to pretend that we are the boy in the story. We'll use our bodies to act out all of the things that the boy does. And we'll act out how his family wags their finger. And at the end, we'll make our bodies into very small seed bodies and grow until we become carrots with green fluffy tops.

Your job is to use your bodies, not your voice. I'll be the person telling the story.

First, we need to spread out in this area. Find a space in the room. Extend your arms out to the side like a windmill or a helicopter. Slowly and gently turn around. Make sure you aren't in anyone else's playing space so you don't bump into each other during our play.

Drama activities for young children work best when there is a clear beginning and end to the activity. To begin, the media specialist says, "Let's get ready to enter the world of the story called *The Carrot Seed.*" At the same time, she swirls her arms above her head, the same gesture used for the imagination feature of the Welcoming Ritual. The children are encouraged to join in speaking this line.

The media specialist then begins telling the story, preferably summarizing from memory so she, too, can participate in the pantomime. As the story progresses, everyone in the class mimes the activities of the boy as they are spoken by the media specialist: digging a hole for the seed; opening the seed packet; and selecting, planting, and watering a seed. The class wags its fingers as the text describes how the family members try to convince him that the seed won't grow. These actions are repeated when they are repeated in the text.

Finally, when the carrot seed grows, the students become the seed, moving from small, seed-shaped bodies to kneeling, to standing upright, with arms above their heads. (The "Tall, Small, Wide, Skinny" warm-up from chapter 2 is helpful, as this vocabulary can coach students into more exaggerated and specific movements.)

Concluding the Unison Pantomime

At the conclusion of the pantomime, the media specialist signals the end by swirling her arms above her head in the "imagination" gesture and saying, "And *that* is the end of the story called *The Carrot Seed.*"

Unison Pantomime Extension

Some stories can grow beyond unison pantomime if students are ready. *The Carrot Seed* is a good example of this. If the initial level of unison pantomime is successful, the story could be repeated, this time dividing the class into two groups. Half of the students are the seed, squatting with small bodies throughout the book and growing at the end, and the other half remain the little boy. Arrange the "boys" in a circle and place the "seeds" inside the circle. If done this way, count the number of "seeds" inside the circle and have the "boys" count and pantomime planting an identical number of seeds from their imaginary seed packets. If splitting the class in half is successful, the exercise can be expanded again, dividing the class into thirds: one-third as boys, one-third as doubting family members, and one-third as seeds.

Unison Pantomime Assessment

Unison pantomime can be an ungraded exploratory activity. However, if assessment is required or preferred, keep in mind that it can be difficult for an instructor to both lead this improvisational activity and simultaneously score it. If working alone, consider taking Kelner and Flynn's advice (2006) and evaluating only a handful of students during each class. This will make more in-depth observation possible. A running record checklist, like the sheet on page 39, can help instructors track each student's progress. Because each student's progress is marked on the same sheet, instructors can also identify classwide areas of strength or weakness and adjust warm-up and main lesson activities accordingly.

Student Name	Date/Project:	Body Expressiveness	Vocal Expressiveness	Imaginative Interpretation	Concentration and Focus	Cooperation/Working Together	Date/Project:	Body Expressiveness	Vocal Expressiveness	Imaginative Interpretation	Concentration and Focus	Cooperation/Working Together	Date/Project:	Body Expressiveness	Vocal Expressiveness	Imaginative Interpretation	Concentration and Focus	Cooperation/Working Together	
1																			
2																			
3																			
4																			
5																			
6																			
7																			
8																			
9																			
10																			
11																			
12																			
13																			
14																			
15																			

If partnering with a classroom teacher, consider having one instructor lead the activity while the other supports the instruction and observes the students. This allows for more focused observations and perhaps the addition of a few narrative sentences.

Stories to Try with Unison Pantomime

Beaumont, Karen. *I Ain't Gonna Paint No More!* Illustrated by David Catrow. Orlando, FL: Harcourt, 2005. unpaged. ISBN 0152024883.

Grades: Pre-K–K

Summary: A child just can't stop painting himself/herself until every body part is dripping with paint! Set to a familiar folk tune.

Unison Role: The child

Tips: Create a gesture that is repeated each time the refrain is said, perhaps shaking a finger in front of the body accompanied by a shaking of the head. Point to each body part as it is mentioned. This is a fast story, so you will want to have another activity lined up in case the pantomime finishes early.

Carle, Eric. *The Tiny Seed.* New York: Simon & Schuster, 1995. unpaged. ISBN 0887080154.

Grades: K–1

Summary: A tiny seed survives many challenges and grows into a flowering plant. The story demonstrates the life cycle of a seed/flower.

Unison Role: The tiny seed

Tips: This is an excellent narrative pantomime to reinforce listening comprehension. On most pages, something happens to most seeds, but it *doesn't* happen to the tiniest seed. If desired, appoint a "book holder" to hold up the illustrations as a visual reinforcement of what the children should be enacting.

Rosen, Michael. *We're Going on a Bear Hunt.* Illustrated by Helen Oxenbury. New York: Margaret K. McElderry, 1989. unpaged. ISBN 0689504764.

Grades: Pre-K–1

Summary: In Rosen's rendition of the classic childhood chant, a family goes hunting for bears, but when they find one, they run home.

Unison Role: Everyone in the class portrays one of the family members. They mime walking over, under, around, and through various obstacles.

Tips: This book and unison pantomime move quickly; consider pairing this with another story or activity.

Rosenthal, Amy Krouse. *Little Pea*. San Francisco: Chronicle Books, 2005. unpaged. ISBN 081184658X.

      Grades: Pre-K–K

    Summary: Little Pea loves playing with his food. However, when mealtime comes, he is required to eat a despised food—candy—in order to qualify for dessert: spinach!

  Unison Role: Little Pea

        Tips: Count each of the five eaten pieces of candy aloud. This brief story, like *The Carrot Seed,* can be repeated, this time with the class divided into three roles: Mama Pea, Papa Pea, and Little Pea.

Saunders-Smith, Gail. *Rain*. Mankato, Minn.: Pebble Books, 1998. 24p. ISBN 1560657782.

      Grades: K–2

    Summary: This nonfiction book with simple text describes the cycle that makes rain fall.

  Unison Role: Water in the water cycle

        Tips: This book is very small in size; consider using a document camera or opaque projector so it can be seen easily by all. Discussion of the water cycle prior to acting it out will strengthen the impact of the activity.

■ ENSEMBLE PANTOMIME

Most stories have multiple characters and are not suited for the unison pantomime technique described above. They are better enacted when students take on individual and different roles. I call this "ensemble pantomime," meaning that a different student is assigned to each role discussed in the book, creating an "ensemble." An ensemble is a group of performers who work together, each with his or her own musical or theatrical part, to create a work.

The remaining children are the "audience." An audience is the group of people who observe the performance, reacting and responding to the performers. In ensemble pantomime, the audience provides sound effects and the repetitive phrases practiced during storytime. As in unison pantomime, the instructor remains the narrator.

Choosing a Story for Ensemble Pantomime

When evaluating whether or not a story will work for ensemble pantomime, consider the following questions:

- Is there a lot of action in the plot (versus a lot of description or a character's interior thoughts)?

- Are there enough characters so that at least 20 percent of the class will have a part?

- Are there interesting sound effects, songs, or repeated phrases in the story (or that can be added easily) that will keep the audience engaged?

- Will the story work without props or scenery?

A list of recommended ensemble pantomime stories is at the end of this section.

To illustrate the steps of ensemble pantomime, "A Good Night's Sleep," an adaptation of the Russian folktale "Peace and Quiet," is used (see page 43). Please read this text prior to moving forward in the chapter.

A Good Night's Sleep
A Russian Folktale Adapted by Kristin Fontichiaro

Tatiana and Ilena were two sisters who lived together in a tiny little house at the top of a tiny hill.

Each night, Tatiana and Ilena would fold back the covers on their beds, say good night, and fall fast asleep. Until one night came when they could not sleep a wink. The tree scratched against the window. The wind whistled down the chimney. And the floor boards creaked.

"I can't sleep!" said Tatiana. "Neither can I," said Ilena. "The tree and the wind and the floor boards are too noisy." And so they lay there awake, all night long.

In the morning, the two sisters were very cranky and tired.

"We have to get some sleep!" said Ilena.

"But how?" said Tatiana. "I can't sleep a wink with the tree and the wind and the floorboards."

"We'll have to ask Mikhail," said Ilena. "He's the smartest man in the village."

And so Ilena and Tatiana left their house, closing the door tightly behind them, and walked to Mikhail's house.

"Mikhail!" they called. "We need your help!"

Mikhail opened his door and let them in. "What is the matter?"

"We can't sleep at all! The tree is scratching against the window, the wind is whistling down the chimney, and the floor boards are creaking!"

"I know just what you should do," said Mikhail. "Bring your cat inside for the night."

That night, before they went to bed, they brought the cat inside. Then they folded back the covers on their beds, said good night, and tried to fall fast asleep. But they couldn't! The cat meowed and meowed. Tatiana and Ilena lay there awake, all night long.

"We have to ask Mikhail for some more advice," said Ilena. "He's the smartest man in the village."

"Mikhail!" they called. "We need your help!"

Mikhail opened his door and let them in. "What is the matter?"

"We can't sleep at all! The cat was up meowing all night long!"

"I know just what you should do," said Mikhail. "You need another animal. This time, bring your dog and your cat inside for the night."

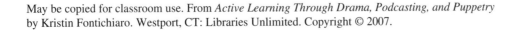

I know just what you should do . . .

That night, before they went to bed, they made sure the cat and the dog were inside the house for the night. Then they folded back the covers on their beds, said good night, and wanted to fall fast asleep. But they couldn't! The cat meowed and meowed and the dog pawed and barked. Tatiana and Ilena lay there awake, all night long.

In the morning, the two sisters were very cranky again. Now they hadn't slept for three nights!

"Mikhail!" they called. "We need your help!"

Mikhail opened his door and let them in. "What is the matter?"

"We can't sleep at all! The cat meowed and meowed, and the dog pawed and barked, all night long!"

"I know just what you should do," said Mikhail. "You need another animal. This time, bring your cat and your dog and your rooster inside for the night."

And so it continued that each night, they brought a new animal into the house until the night came when their cat, dog, rooster, goat, and cow were all inside their tiny little house on the hill. As with every other night, the two sisters couldn't sleep a wink.

At two o'clock in the morning, there was a knock at the door. Of course, Tatiana and Ilena were both wide awake, so they tiptoed to the door to answer it.

Can you guess who was at the door? It was Mikhail!

"Good evening. I was just stopping by and saw your light. Are you not sleeping?"

"Oh, it's awful!" they said. "All these animals make so much noise that we can't sleep a wink!"

"Let me try something," said Mikhail. And one by one, he led the animals outside: the cow and the goat and the rooster and the dog and the cat.

"Whew," said the sisters. "It certainly did get quiet in here."

And, compared to the animals being there, it was. Now all they could hear was the tree scratching gently against the window, the quiet wind in the chimney, and the tiny squeak of the floorboards.

And that is how Tatiana and Ilena finally got a good night's sleep.

Getting Started with Ensemble Pantomime

Ensemble pantomime follows the same process as unison pantomime: Welcoming Ritual, warm-ups, storytime, and the enactment of the story. However, two optional steps may be added prior to the ensemble pantomime reenactment: bringing the students into the planning process and adding sound effects. These activities help children dig deeper into the story and become more alert to sensory details

Bringing Students into the Planning Process

One option that can be added to an ensemble pantomime lesson after reading the story is a brainstorming and planning session. During this time, students work with the instructors to create a list of characters that can serve as a visual reference during the reenactment. This step is recommended if the media center schedule allows up to 45 minutes for a narrative pantomime lesson. If time is more limited, it may be necessary to eliminate this step and proceed directly to pantomiming the story.

If pursuing this discussion time, the media specialist begins by asking students to help brainstorm a list of characters. Each character is written (or drawn for preschool or kindergarten) on a large Post-It™ note. The Post-It is posted on chart paper or white board. Brainstorm a few words that describe each character's personality. Look beyond human characters to include animals, furniture, props, and more.

For example, in the sample text, the brainstormed list might include the following:

- Tatiana
- Ilena (sister of Tatiana)
- Headboards and footboards for the beds
- Mikhail (wise man?) Is he really wise?
- Cat—meows
- Dog—barks
- Rooster—crows and pecks (What is "pecks?"—scratches beak on ground)
- Goat—butts horns
- Cow—moos
- Squeaky door at sister's house
- Door to Mikhail's house

Then ask students to come up and help you sequence the characters. This has two purposes: it strengthens students' sequencing skills and it provides a visual reference while you are re-creating the story.

Identifying the Sound Effects

Next, if time is available, the class brainstorms a list of sound effects that can be provided by the "audience." (Often these are the parts where children joined in during the storytime reading.) If on a fixed schedule with limited time, the media specialist might need to pre-identify these roles. For "A Good Night's Sleep," there are three major sound effect opportunities:

> the scratching tree,
>
> the whistling wind in the chimney, and
>
> the squeaking floor.

The class discusses how the "audience" could all make the sounds for each item, or the audience could be split into thirds, with one-third of the class making each of the sounds. The class decides to split into thirds.

The media specialist then rehearses the sound effects. Like a choral conductor, she explains that she will cue the class when it is time to start and stop. To start, she will stick out her hand with the palm facing up, and to stop, she will raise her hand in the air to signal that it is almost time to end the sound effect. The sound effect stops when the hand closes.

Ground Rules

Before beginning any drama activity, take some time to outline expectations. In many schools, children have not been exposed to drama work and may not know what to expect. They may associate kinesthetic work with recess and need to be reminded that this is learning time, not play time. Reviewing the ground rules gives students confidence that they know what is expected of them.

- Keep your voices quiet when the narrator is speaking.
- Keep your classmates safe.
- The playing space is inside the marked area. (See chapter 2.)
- There are no props or costumes. We use our imagination instead.
- When your character is not onstage, please return to the audience.
- Being a great audience is an important job. Good audience members look at the people who are talking, keep their voices quiet until it's their turn to speak, keep their bodies checked to keep the playing space safe, and enjoy the performers.
- Good audience members laugh at the funny parts (but don't roll all over the floor while they're doing it!).
- Our job is to tell the story the way the author and illustrator told it in the book.
- When it's time for a sound effect, watch for the teacher's hand in the air. When the hand closes, stop the sound effect. (Practice this beforehand.)
- Everyone will get a part, either as an actor or as a member of the audience. The teacher will choose students for roles as new characters are introduced in the story.
- Anyone who is having a tough time controlling his or her body or voice may need to sit out for a while on the chairs in the back.
- The instructor is the narrator and the director. The director's decisions are final. The instructor is the only person who can tell the actors to do something different.

When ground rules have been shared, the students may move to the "audience" area (see the diagram on page 36). Unless the story is complex, leave the book on the storytime chair. If it's a story in which remembering the sequence of events might be difficult for students, or if you need to engage a shy student, ask one student to be the book holder, who holds out the illustrations for other students to refer to during the drama. Remind students to "body check" themselves so their arms and legs are not in the way of students coming and going during the pantomime.

Casting Ensemble Pantomime: Picking Roles and Deciding Who's Who

Choosing students to play particular roles is known as "casting." Traditionally, when casting a play, all of the parts are assigned before beginning the play. Although this certainly works, I prefer a technique presented by Sean Layne (http://www.seanlayne.com), a national workshop presenter for the Kennedy Center. He practices "cast-as-you-go" casting. Instead of casting everyone up front, select the characters who are "on stage" when the play begins. Wait to select students for other roles until new characters are introduced in the story. This keeps all students "tuned in" during the performance.

During early lessons involving ensemble pantomime, it may be advantageous to cast only from the students who volunteer. This helps breed early success: eager participants will make narrative pantomime look fun and easy. If nonvolunteers are assigned roles, they may be too shy to participate or even refuse, stagnating the potential of the activity. Some students need to observe the process before they feel safe engaging in it.

This method helps eliminate disruptive behavior from kids who stand up, arms high in the air, shouting, "Ooh! Ooh! Pick me! Pick me!" Instead, in the "A Good Night's Sleep" example, say,

> Who do we need to begin this play? That's right, we need Tatiana and Ilena. I will know that you want to be Tatiana because you have both hands on top of your head. *(Scan the group for volunteers.)* All right, Jacquie, you may be Tatiana today. Would you please go up to the playing area and get ready? And now we need Ilena. If you would like to be Ilena, you are showing me how tired you are from not being able to sleep. *(Look for volunteers.)* All right, Linda, would you be Ilena today? Please join Tatiana in the playing area.

Notice how casting can be a character-based action—such as auditioning Ilena by asking her to show how tired she is—or a more generic action, such as asking students to "audition" by putting hands on their heads. The rest of the class can be involved as audience members, providing the sound effects outlined earlier.

Of course, not everyone can be the sisters, and those not chosen may initiate a chorus of, "Aw! That's not fair!" Gently remind students that this activity will be repeated many times throughout the year, and students will take turns having special parts. "One way you can show me that you are ready for a special part is by keeping your body in check and your voice in control." Then go on telling the story, casting new characters as they appear in the story.

Action! The Ensemble Pantomime Begins

Now it is time to retell the story as the actors pantomime it. It is time for "Places." In a professional play, the stage manager calls "Places" when it is time for the characters who are onstage when the play begins to take their positions. At "Places," Tatiana and Ilena are onstage.

Next, have a clear beginning by waving your hands above your head (the same gesture used for "imagination" during the Welcoming Ritual) and saying, "Let's get ready to enter the world of the story of 'A Good Night's Sleep'." This reminds students that the story is starting and that it's time to assume their roles.

If the story is new to you, execute your role as narrator by reading directly from the book. This helps to ensure that a character is not left out accidentally. If you know the story very well, you may have it committed to memory, in which case students are often impressed when you tell it in your own words. Working from memory also lets you "tweak" the story and make it more "act-out-able." You can spell out actions to be taken to keep the action moving, trim descriptive passages that would have your actors standing still, and keep the audience alert by subtly altering the words and phrases.

While reading or telling the story, position yourself to the side of the action, with your body turned at a 45 degree angle (as shown on page 36) for a clear view of both the action that is unfolding on the "stage" and the audience, to gauge their reactions and attention.

Because the student actors are just getting used to the story, expect that they will respond to the narration with a slight delay. Pause at key action moments to give them time to react and enact what you have just said. Be sure to pause the narrative when the audience laughs: the "funny parts" are often the moments that children will savor most.

The document on page 48 shows how "A Good Night's Sleep" might play out in the ensemble pantomime style.

(1) Tatiana and Ilena were two sisters who lived together in a tiny little house at the top of a tiny hill.

Each night, Tatiana and Ilena would fold back the covers on their beds, say good night, (2) and fall fast asleep. Until one night came when they could not sleep a wink. (3) The tree scratched against the window. The wind whistled down the chimney. And the floor boards creaked.

"I can't sleep!" said Tatiana. "Neither can I," said Ilena. "The tree and the wind and the floor boards are too noisy." And so they lay there awake, all night long.

In the morning, the two sisters were very cranky and tired.

"We have to get some sleep!" said Ilena.

"But how?" said Tatiana. "I can't sleep a wink with the tree and the wind and the floorboards."

"We'll have to ask Mikhail," said Ilena. "He's the smartest man in the village." (4)

And so Ilena and Tatiana left their house, closing the door tightly behind them, and walked to Mikhail's house. (5)

"Mikhail!" they called. "We need your help!"

Mikhail opened his door and let them in. "What is the matter?"

"We can't sleep at all! The tree is scratching against the window, the wind is whistling down the chimney, and the floor boards are creaking!"

"I know just what you should do," said Mikhail. "Bring your cat inside for the night. (6)

That night, before they went to bed, (7) they brought the cat inside. Then they folded back the covers on their beds, said good night, and tried to fall fast asleep. But they couldn't! The cat meowed and meowed. (7) Tatiana and Ilena lay there awake, all night long.

"We have to ask Mikhail for some more advice," said Ilena. "He's the smartest man in the village."

"Mikhail!" they called. "We need your help!"

Mikhail opened his door and let them in. "What is the matter?"

"We can't sleep at all! The cat was up meowing all night long!"

(8) "I know just what you should do," said Mikhail. "You need another animal. This time, bring your dog and your cat inside for the night. (9)

That night, before they went to bed, they made sure the cat and the dog were inside the house for the night. Then they folded back the covers on their beds, said good night, and wanted to fall fast asleep. But they couldn't! The cat meowed and meowed and the dog pawed and barked. (10) Tatiana and Ilena lay there awake, all night long.

In the morning, the two sisters were very cranky again. Now they hadn't slept for three nights!

"Mikhail!" they called. "We need your help!"

Mikhail opened his door and let them in. "What is the matter?"

"We can't sleep at all! The cat meowed and meowed, and the dog pawed and barked, all night long!"

(8) "I know just what you should do," said Mikhail. "You need another animal. This time, bring your cat and your dog and your rooster inside for the night."

(11) And so it continued that each night, they brought a new animal into the house until the night came when their cat, dog, rooster, goat, and cow were all inside their tiny little house on the hill. As with every other night, the two sisters couldn't sleep a wink.

At two o'clock in the morning, there was a knock at the door. (11) Of course, Tatiana and Ilena were both wide awake, so they tiptoed to the door to answer it.

Can you guess who was at the door? It was Mikhail!

"Good evening. I was just stopping by and saw your light. Are you not sleeping?"

"Oh, it's awful!" they said. "All these animals make so much noise that we can't sleep a wink!"

"Let me try something," said Mikhail. (12) And one by one, he led the animals outside: the cow and the goat and the rooster and the dog and the cat. (12)

"Whew," said the sisters. "It certainly did get quiet in here."

And, compared to the animals being there, it was! (13) Now all they could hear was the tree scratching gently against the window, the quiet wind in the chimney, and the tiny squeak of the floorboards.

And that is how Tatiana and Ilena finally got a good night's sleep. (13)

---

1. Review Ground Rules. Ask, "Who is onstage when we start?" Practice signaling with sound effects; make sure each audience group knows which sound effect it is assigned to make. Define the playing space. Set up two pairs of chairs, one for each bed. Say, "Let's get ready to enter the world of the story called "A Good Night's Sleep."

2. Pause between each item to give students time to respond.

3. Cue each audience group to enter by pointing to them. At end of paragraph, close hand to signal that sound effects should stop.

4. Say to audience, "What should happen next?" Then cast two people to make the door." "You can show me you want to be the door by showing how strong you are."

5. Cast Mikhail's door (see Step 4).

6. There is nothing in the text about going home, so add some to help the actors: "Mikhail went back inside his house. They went home and opened the door." Cast the cat by saying, "You can show me you want to be cat by showing me your whiskers." Mikhail can wait at the edge of the stage for his next scene.

7. Say to audience, "What do you suppose that sounds like?" and hold out hand. Close it after a few seconds to stop the sound.

8. Ask audience, "What do you think he will tell them to do?"

9. Ask audience to predict whether or not this will work. Then cast the dog: "If you would like to be the dog, show me your wagging tail."

10. Repeat the pattern from earlier in the story.

10. Expand the text to repeat the pattern, casting the rooster, goat, and cow with each new repetition.

11. Say to audience, "What did that knock sound like?" End sound by closing hand.

12. As animals leave scene, gesture for them to rejoin the audience.

13. Say, "And THAT was the end of the story called 'A Good Night's Sleep.'"

Coaching Students into More Physically Engaged Movement

Sometimes students are shy and they seem to "just stand there" instead of enthusiastically assuming a character role. Do not be afraid to augment the story with action clues that can jumpstart behavior. For example, if using P. D. Eastman's classic *Are You My Mother?* the instructor might say to the child playing the baby bird, "Let's see what the baby bird looked like in his egg. Can you show me a small body?" To the children playing the Snort, one might say, "How can you make your bodies look more like a Snort? Would a tall body for the shovel and a small body for the wheels help it look more realistic?" To the children playing the airplane, the prompt might be, "Can you show us what the plane might look like flying overhead?" and to the children playing the boat, "The boat was down, down, down. Can you use your bodies to show us what those down, down, down boats might look like? Should you be as tall as the baby bird, or can you make yourself lower?"

Ending the Play

Having a concrete ending for the play is as important as having a clearly defined beginning. As at the beginning of the play, repeat the waving arms from the Welcoming Ritual as you say, "And THAT was the end of the story called 'A Good Night's Sleep'." Especially as this technique is introduced to students, it is useful to remind them that this is the *end* of the playing time: that students are no longer trolls or bears or Goldilocks or monkeys.

Assessment

Ensemble pantomime can be an ungraded exploratory activity. However, if assessment is desired, consider evaluating a few students during each visit using the running record (page 39) or by asking students to reflect and self-evaluate using a combination of the following questions. Notice how the questions relate to the five skills of the Welcoming Ritual.

1. How did I use my *body* to tell the story (if an actor)?
2. How did I use my *voice* to tell the story (if a member of the audience)?
3. How did I use my *imagination* to bring the story to life?
4. How could others tell that I was *concentrating* during the narrative pantomime?
5. How could others tell that I was *cooperating* during the narrative pantomime?

Stories for Ensemble Pantomime (Grades K–3)

Hundreds of stories can be retold using the ensemble pantomime techniques. The following list of folktales that translate well to ensemble pantomime is merely a starting point. Some of the stories come from story collections, in which there are few illustrations. Students can listen raptly to stories—especially folktales—told aloud without the benefit of illustrations. It may seem counterintuitive to say that twenty-first-century students are *more* attentive when there is *less* stimulation, but try it. You might be surprised!

> "The Princess and the Pea"
>
> Anansi stories
>
> "The House That Jack Built"
>
> "The Three Billy Goats Gruff"
>
> "I Know an Old Lady Who Swallowed a Fly"
>
> "Cinderella"
>
> "Sleeping Beauty"
>
> Stories from *Aesop's Fables* (choose two or three to fill a single class period)

The stories listed below come from picture books. Since many stories for early elementary children rely on illustration to portray character, picture book illustrations can often help jumpstart conversations about character.

Adler, Naomi. "The Monkey's Heart." In *The Barefoot Book of Animal Tales*. Illustrated by Amanda Hall. Cambridge, MA: Barefoot Books, 1996. 80pp. ISBN184686013X.

> **Grades:** 1–3
>
> **Summary:** In this African folktale, Monkey lives in a mango tree and shares its bounty with many of his friends, including Crocodile, who takes many fruits back to his chief and tribe. The chief decides that the heart from a mango-fed monkey would be a great delicacy and tricks Crocodile into kidnapping Monkey. When they are descending into the river, Monkey complains that he cannot swim, and Crocodile confesses to his plan to surrender Monkey's heart to his chief. Monkey tricks Crocodile into believing that he keeps his heart in the mango tree and escapes.
>
> **Roles Needed:** Monkey, Crocodile, Crocodile chief, tree branches, waves
>
> **Tips:** This story takes place in a tree, on the ground, and deep in the water. To create a sense of height, use sturdy chairs for the monkey to stand on and invite a few students to surround the chair to create branches. A few students portray the river's waves. (Consider long pieces of cloth held by students to portray the waves.) Sound effects for the audience include the lapping water and the licking of the crocodile chief's lips.

Matthews, Caitlin. "The Horned Snake's Wife." In *The Barefoot Book of Princesses*. Cambridge, MA: Barefoot Books, 1997. 63pp. 1841481726 (pbk.).

> **Grades:** 4–5
>
> **Summary:** An Iroquois chief and his wife wish their daughter to marry, but she finds fault in all of her suitors. When a mysterious warrior prince arrives, she is magically drawn to him. She and the

prince leave her home, arriving at a riverside hut that smells like rotten fish. She refuses to put on the dress he gives her. The next day, a snake creeps into the lodge; she recognizes it as her fiancé. Had she put on the dress, she would have become a snake as well. Although frightened, she sleeps deeply, dreaming of an old ancestor, who helps her escape The daughter learns to be satisfied with simple things, marries an ordinary man, and becomes wise in her old age. In this story collection, another good story for narrative pantomime is "The Princess and the Pea."

Roles Needed: Chief, Chief's wife, Chief's daughter, Warrior Prince/Snake, several other snakes, Heno the Thunderer (could be played by several students)

Tips: Begin by casting a chief, the chief's wife, the daughter, and several suitors. Pantomime many suitors coming in front of the royal family and being turned away. Then cast the snake prince. Have the audience make the sound of the river as the couple travel. When the daughter awakens the second day, let the audience temporarily become the hissing snakes. To create a sense of the ancestor's greatness, ask three students to work together to make his form and voice. The audience can also supply the drumming sounds of thunder. At the conclusion, the audience can represent members of the village. Finally, cast the daughter's singing spouse and their children.

Martin, Rafe. *The Rough-Face Girl.* Illustrated by David Shannon. New York: G. P. Putnam, 1992. unpaged. ISBN 0399218599.

Grades: 3–4

Summary: Two cruel sisters taunt their sister, the Rough-Face Girl, as they compete to win the hand of Invisible Being.

Roles Needed: Invisible Being, sister of Invisible Being (perhaps one child to be the sister and two additional children to pop up when her voice booms), poor father, his two cruel daughters, Rough-Face Girl, several children to form Rough-Face Girl's wigwam and the wigwam of Invisible Being, two children to portray the fire. Optional: children to portray the lakeshore, the bow and arrows, the rainbow, setting sun, glittering stars. Use the audience to act as the villagers and react to the older sisters as they flaunt their new clothing.

Tips: As a class, decide how to portray Invisible Being: should he be portrayed by an actor or kept invisible in the sky? Should he be seen in the wigwam? At the end? Allow 20 minutes to retell this story.

Matthews, John. "Oona and the Giant." In *The Barefoot Book of Giants, Ghosts, and Goblins: Traditional Tales from Around the World.* Cambridge, MA: Barefoot Books, 1999. 80pp. ISBN 1902283279.

Grades: 2–4

Summary: This Irish tale, also known as "Finn McCool" or "Fionn Mac Cool," tells the story of how Oona, the clever wife of Fionn the Giant, saves her husband from a confrontation with the even more giant Cuchalainn. Fionn, who can see anything in the world just by sucking his thumb, knows Cuchalainn is headed for their home. Oona hides Fionn in a baby cradle, then springs into action, challenging Cuchalainn to amazing feats until, worn down, Cuchalainn goes to greet the "baby," who bites Cuchalainn's finger and saps him of his giant size and strength. With a female protagonist as the mastermind behind the plot, this story brings excellent gender balance to any folktale unit. Another good narrative pantomime story in this collection is "The Drinking Companions," a tale from China.

Roles Needed: Fionn, Oona, Cuchalainn

Tips: Discuss voice volume with the actors. How does voice help us know that a character is big? How would Cuchalainn move differently from us? Audience sound effects can include the sound of biting into the stony scone.

Rathmann, Peggy. *Officer Buckle and Gloria.* New York: Putnam, 1995. unpaged. ISBN 0399226168.

Grades: 1–3

Summary: See summary in the introduction to this chapter.

Roles Needed: Officer Buckle, Gloria, principal, students

Tips: Consider excerpting portions of this story, as it is a long narrative. Use sturdy chairs for Officer Buckle's desk and for the principal to stand on. Discuss how to keep the performance safe during the scene in which many accidents happen.

Salley, Coleen. *Why Epossumondas Has No Hair on His Tail.* Illustrated by Janet Stevens. San Diego: Harcourt, 2004. unpaged. ISBN 0152049355.

Grades: 1–2

Summary: This Southern tale explains why Epossumondas the possum has a long, hairless tail. Why, thinks Epossumondas, do so many animals have beautiful and bushy tails, and his own is so skinny and bare? His Mama tells him of his ancestor Papapossum, who awakened one day yearning for persimmons. Hare encouraged him to climb Bear's persimmons tree for them. When Bear caught Papapossum in the act of thievery, he chased Papapossum off his property. As Papapossum got caught in the fence, Bear grabbed onto his tail until it was stretched and hairless. That, says Mama, is why Epossumondas has no hair on his tail.

Roles Needed: Epossumondas, Skunk, Mama, Papapossum, Hare, Bear

Tips: Define the word *persimmons* prior to doing this story. Place a chair on the right side of the stage that can serve as Epossumondas's porch swing, Mama's chair, Papapossum's bed, the persimmon tree, and back to Mama's chair again. To make the change of scenes clear to students, add a few transition sentences, such as, "And now we are in Mama's house. She is sitting on her chair." Set the persimmons song to a simple musical tune and teach it to the audience during storytime to have the greatest possible audience interaction. Students love acting out this story as well as Salley's earlier tale, *Epossumondas.* Consider teaching them in back-to-back lessons.

Sierra, Judy. "Clever Mandy." In *Silly and Sillier.* Illustrated by Valeri Gorbachev. New York: Alfred A. Knopf, 2002. 96pp. ISBN 0375806091.

Grades: 1–2

Summary: This Bahamian variant of "Rumplestiltskin" features a young girl named Mandy, who leaves home to make her way in the world. She meets an old woman who offers a deal: if Mandy works in her house for a year and follows all instructions, the woman will give her half of her treasure. Mandy does so, but when the time comes to collect the treasure, the old woman gives her a new challenge: to win half the treasure, Mandy must discover the old woman's name. The home's cat and dog don't tell, but the crab finds a backhanded way to give Mandy the information. Mandy wins the treasure, but the crab is punished with a swat of the old woman's stick, giving it the hard shell it still has today.

Roles Needed: Mandy, the old woman, the cat, the dog, the crab

Tips: The audience can participate by providing sound effects as Mandy travels from animal to animal, a "thwack" when the old woman hits the crab, and by calling out the old woman's real name on cue. Many other tales in this volume make great narrative pantomimes.

Spinelli, Eileen. *Somebody Loves You, Mr. Hatch.* Illustrated by Paul Yalowitz. New York: Bradbury Press, 1991. unpaged. ISBN 0027860159.

Grades: K–2

Summary: Mr. Hatch receives an unexpected valentine but is not sure who it is from.

Roles Needed: Mr. Hatch, Mr. Smith the newsstand vendor, the butcher Mr. Todd, Mr. Goober the postman, woman tripping over dog, man falling off ladder, girl spilling toys out of wagon, Mr. Todd's daughter Melanie. Students in the audience can join in, acting as the crowd and "watching" as Mr. Hatch goes on the street and reacting with surprise when they see him happy. They can stand to attend the picnic, eat brownies, and drink lemonade. They can talk together about what might be wrong with Mr. Hatch. Optional roles: headboard and footboard of Mr. Hatch's bed, two children to be the newsstand kiosk, one child to be the box of valentine candy.

Tips: Allow extra time (about 20 minutes) for this story.

Stojic, Manya. *Rain.* New York: Crown, 2000. unpaged. ISBN 0517800861.

Grades: Pre-K–1

Summary: The African savanna is hot and parched. The animals, in turn, use the five senses to anticipate the arrival of rain.

Roles Needed: trees (first dry, then sprouting), porcupine, zebras, baboons, rhino, lion, flowers, and the water hole

Tips: Assign several children to play each role. Consider using a flannel board to help children know the sequence of characters. Animals use various senses to know that it is going to rain. Ask the audience to imagine the dry, cracked earth that is the book's opening setting using the five senses, then to use their voices to create a sound for that weather. Repeat the activity later in the play, when the rain turns everything lush and green. Other sound effects for the audience are thunder and rain. Rehearse the cue for sound effects to stop (closing of the instructor's hand).

Wheeler, Lisa. *Farmer Dale's Red Pickup Truck.* Illustrated by Ivan Bates. San Diego: Harcourt, 2004. 40pp. ISBN 0152023194.

Grades: Pre-K–1

Summary: Farmer Dale is driving his pickup truck. One at a time, he meets animals who are blocking his path on the road. He invites them to ride into town with him in his truck. When the truck is so full of animals that it won't go, they get out, push, and help him get his truck going again.

Roles Needed: Farmer Dale, Bossy Cow, Woolly Sheep, Roly Pig, Nanny Goat, Cocky Rooster

Tips: Consider setting up several chairs to make the "truck." The children playing animals can sit in the chairs (much safer than their natural instinct to sit atop one another, which is a more literal interpretation). It also makes it easier to denote the difference between "inside" and "outside" the truck.

Wheeler, Lisa. *Old Cricket.* Illustrated by Ponder Goembel. New York: Richard Jackson/Atheneum, 2003. 32pp. ISBN 1416918558.

Grades: 2–4

Summary: Old Cricket pretends to be sick in order to get out of the work his wife and friends ask him to do. Each believes his faked illness and gives him something to eat on the journey to see the doctor. When Crow arrives to eat him for lunch, Crow doesn't believe his story, and Old Cricket has to use the foods he has been to try to keep Crow at bay.

Roles Needed: Old Cricket, his wife, Katydid, six unnamed ants, Uncle Ant, Old Crow (played by two students standing together, holding their arms out as wings), and Doc Hopper

Tips: Ask the audience to make the creak, crick, hic, and caw noises noted in italics in the story. Create a "traveling tune" that the audience sings each time Old Cricket leaves a friend and continues on his journey. For example, the following traveling music could be sung to the tune of "Pop Goes the Weasel": "I don't feel like working today. I'd like to take a break! I'll trick my friends and say that I'm sore. It's a piece of cake!" This musical interlude keeps the audience engaged throughout the story.

Extension 1: Giving Every Student a Part

To engage all students in a dramatic retelling of a story requires finding enough parts for everyone. Giving everyone a role ignites intrinsic motivation and reduces behavior problems. Belonging and participating feels good and gives students greater ownership over the project.

Many lower elementary classes have 24 to 30 children, but most books for this age group do not have that many characters. How is it possible for everyone to have a part? The answer is to think creatively *beyond* a simple list of the characters in the story.

For example, what important items need to be present that could be role-played by a student? What furniture and scenery are necessary? Children can play these "roles" as well.

Another option is to consider "multiple casting." Multiple casting is a term that refers to assigning more than one actor to play a single part.

Method	Example
Have one student play the body of a character and have the other play the voice.	*Caps for Sale:* One student says, "You monkeys, you! You give me back my caps!" while the other shakes his or her fist.
Have two or more of each character.	*The Mitten:* Instead of having one bear, have two or three.
Have many students work together to create a single item.	*Caps for Sale:* Ask three students to intertwine their arms to create a single large tree.

As an example of how multiple casting techniques can be used, consider the example of "Goldilocks and the Three Bears." The traditional story has only four characters: Goldilocks, Papa Bear, Mama Bear, and Baby Bear. Following are some ways to find a role for each person in a class of 25 students.

Role	Number of Students Needed	Notes
Goldilocks	2	Change the story so it has two Goldilocks girls, not one.
Baby Bear	1	
Mama Bear	1	
Papa Bear	1	
Cottage Door	2	Students can stand shoulder to shoulder to make a very wide door, making a creaking noise whenever the door opens and closes.
Table for Porridge	2	Two children stand back-to-back and then bend at the waist, creating the table top with their backs.
Chair at Table	1	Stand straight up; hold out arms like an armchair. Goldilocks will "sit" by crouching in front of it. Bowls of porridge can be mimed. If class size is very large, three children can stand behind the table to be bowls of porridge.
Papa and Mama's Easy Chairs	2 per chair; total of 4	Created similarly to the table chair. However, to show how massive it is, two students can stand shoulder-to-shoulder.
Baby Bear's Easy Chair	1	Same as Chair at Table.

Role	Number of Students Needed	Notes
Headboards for Papa and Mama's Beds	2 for each; total of 4	Two kids stand erect and shoulder-to-shoulder.
Footboards for Papa and Mama's Beds	2 for each; total of 4	Two kids kneel to create footboard. To "lie in bed," Goldilocks lies on the floor between the headboard and footboard.
Baby Bear's Headboard (1) and Footboard (1)	2	One person stands erect. It is the smallest bed, so it only requires one person for its headboard!
TOTAL:	**25 roles**	

▶ *Keeping Track of the Characters*

Plot out the number and potential types of roles in advance to be sure the story is workable, even if students will be led in brainstorming a list of characters as part of the lesson. Although children may create a slightly different list, knowing that a story can accommodate many students in the class will help create a successful kickoff to the activity.

Unless it is a very familiar story, it may be helpful to post a cheat sheet where you can refer to it. Cheat sheets can be big or small. Type up a list of characters and the number of students needed to portray each character. For a large guide, use 60-point type or larger and tape the printout to the end of a bookshelf where you can see it from a distance. Another option is to type up the information using small type and tape it to the back side of a staff ID badge. Try not to carry a piece of paper so that your hands remain free for other tasks.

Once you have done this type of work a few times, your brain will automatically begin to adapt. You will find yourself thinking, "Hmmm . . . I'm going to need to have four lions here, or I won't have anyone left for the end!"

Extension 2: Giving Students a Voice—Adding Dialogue and Engagement to the Play

▶ *Keeping the "Offstage" Students Involved*

To keep the audience engaged, involve them in questioning as the play progresses. In "The Three Billy Goats Gruff," for example, pause to ask the audience, "Who came across the bridge first?" to build sequencing skills. Another idea is to say to the uncast students remaining on the sidelines, "Show us with your faces what kind of person the troll was . . . good! Now add a sound that you think matches the troll," to informally assess student understanding of character. Doing this periodically keeps the "offstage" students more engaged and attentive.

▶ Coaching and Cuing Young Performers for Dialogue

With the youngest students, the media specialist will not only narrate the story but speak the character's lines as well. As student confidence grows, the performers will begin to speak along with the instructor. The instructor can pause to allow the student to attempt the next line of dialogue on his or her own. If the student is able to speak without prompting, the level of the activity has just risen. The instructor knows the student is ready to take additional responsibility for his or her character interpretation. If the student falters or does not respond, try saying, "Let's listen to what she said," then wait for a response. If there is still no response, say, "Would you like me to say it with you?" and begin to speak the line along with the child. As time goes on, your ability to correctly predict the amount of support a child needs will improve.

As students become more comfortable, they may assume complete ownership of the story reenactment, no longer pausing for the instructor to provide narrative. This is an exciting instructional moment, because it means that students have crossed over into independent learning.

▶ Keeping Dialogue True to the Original Story

Expect that the actors will respond in a way that is aligned with the story. If a child gives an answer that is out of place, say, "Today our job is to retell the author's version of the story. Your version would be good for your writing journal. Let's try this again." If a student remains silly, ask him or her to sit in a chair for a while until he or she feels ready to come back.

■ CIRCLE DRAMA

Circle drama is a more sophisticated version of narrative pantomime that works best with lower elementary students. I've termed this method "circle drama" because with it, students create a playing space by sitting or standing in the same circle (or taped square) used for the Welcoming Ritual. There is no clear separation between actor and audience. Playing "in the round," with students on all sides of the playing space, provides a nurturing, cozy environment that lowers student anxiety. Each student has a part, and student voices are engaged. Circle drama is adapted from observations of the work of Lenore Blank Kelner and Sean Layne and from the work of Viola Spolin.

As in narrative pantomime, there are four steps to circle drama: Welcoming Ritual, storytime, warm-ups, and circle drama. Refer to chapter 2 for possible Welcoming Rituals. Follow the instructions from earlier in the chapter for the Welcoming Ritual, storytime, and warm-ups.

When ready to begin the circle drama, ask the students to sit on the circle shape and review the ground rules established earlier. Use the same methods of multiple casting and questioning the audience and characters. Take advantage of the defined playing space and use it as a "home base" for actors when not on the stage. Be sure to ask students to "body check" so performers do not trip over arms or legs.

With circle drama, students expect a role. Sometimes, when nearing the end of the play, it may become evident that everyone has been "holding out" and waiting for a certain part. For example, in "The Enormous Turnip," many children wish to be the mouse or cricket whose small action, combined with everyone's effort, finally yanks the resistant turnip out of the ground. Enthusiasm may be high as students volunteer for earlier roles like the grandfather and the grandmother in the story, but that enthusiasm may wane as many children sit on their hands in hopes (and, with young children, the *belief*) that they will get to be the mouse. There may be no volunteers for these "middle parts." Do not be afraid to assign roles to children. Again, remind them that they will be repeating this activity, and they may get their first choice another time. A student may say, "I don't WANT to be the dog!" If this occurs, try giving the child a choice. Say, "How about a choice? You may be the dog, or you may sit out and watch," or, "You may be the dog, or you may be the cat." Most children, given a choice, will drop their complaint and become part of the ensemble. Avoid the urge to give in to a sulking child, or the students will learn that when they protest, you will recast the play (and imagine how that feels to the child whose part has been taken away!).

If students continue to express displeasure, you might say, "You know? You could tell this story again your own way when you go out for recess today, but for now, we're going to try it this way."

For some plays, you may wish to cast by going around the circle. For example, with "For Sale," you might say, "I will pick four people to be monkeys with blue caps. As I tap you on the head, please go and get a cap from the peddler's head." Then choose the first four available students. Choose the next four students in the circle to be the next monkey with the next color cap, and so on. This makes casting more efficient and, in the students' eyes, more objective.

Circle Drama Assessment

Use the reading record (page 39) or the narrative pantomime student questions (page 49) for assessment.

Books Suitable for Circle Drama

▶ *Folktales*

"The Enormous Turnip"

"Henny Penny/Chicken Little"

"The Little Red Hen"

"The Mitten/The Woodcutter's Cap"

"Peace and Quiet"

"Stone Soup"

▶ *Picture Books*

Brett, Jan. *The Hat.* New York: Putnam, 1997. unpaged. ISBN 0399231013.

> **Grades:** 1–2
>
> **Summary:** As Hedgie the hedgehog travels around the farm, the animals make fun of him for wearing Lisa's sock as a hat. When Lisa removes the sock and returns it to the laundry line, she discovers that the other animals have helped themselves to something to wear!
>
> **Roles Needed:** Lisa, her storage chest (two children), clothes hanging on line (several children in the center of the circle or all children who at that moment have no part, standing on the tape line posed like clothing on the line), stocking/hat, hen, her chicks, gander, barn cat, farm dog, dog's puppies, mother pig, piglets, pony
>
> **Tips:** Use a flannel board or other visual device to help students remember the order of the animals visited. During the "Make Me a . . ." warm-up, suggest objects that help children practice the limp body shapes to prepare for re-creating the clothing on the line. Examples: "Make me a flag on a flagpole on a day with no wind," or, "Make me a blanket being dragged by a baby."

Bryan, Ashley. *Beautiful Blackbird.* New York: Atheneum, 2003. unpaged. ISBN 0689847319.

> **Grades:** 3–4
>
> **Summary:** In this Zambian tale, Blackbird is the only bird with black feathers. The other birds, including Ringdove, admire Blackbird's feathers and dance and chant about his beauty. Finally, Ringdove convinces Blackbird to paint a black ring around his neck so that his name will match his appearance. Blackbird warns the other birds that just painting black on them will not make them just like him, but that black creates a beautiful appearance. This book was awarded the 2004 Coretta Scott King Illustrator Award.
>
> **Roles Needed:** Blackbird, Ringdove, two or three children to make the medicine gourd. The rest of the class plays the other birds.
>
> **Tips:** There are many kinds of birds in the story. Consider adding a "Make Me a . . ." warm-up: ask children to make a bird. Say, "Now make me a different kind of bird . . . a tall bird . . . a small bird . . . a bird that doesn't fly." Invite the other students to stand around the circle and be the other birds in the story. For the chanted parts, consider using some of the choral techniques explained in chapter 8. Students could break into small groups,

with each responsible for turning one of the chants into an interesting choral reading. Rehearse the refrain with the class during storytime.

Chamberlin, Mary, and Rich Chamberlin. *Mama Panya's Pancakes: A Village Tale from Kenya.* Cambridge, MA: Barefoot Books, 2005. unpaged. ISBN 184481394.

Grades: 2–3

Summary: On their way to market, Mama Panya's son invites all they meet to join them at home for pancakes. Mama Panya worries that she will not have enough for everyone, but Adika reminds her that she has enough for "a little bit and a little bit more." At the end, all arrive at Mama Panya's, bringing enough ingredients so that all can eat.

Roles Needed: Mama Panya, Adika, Mzee Odolo (fishing), Sawandi and Naiman (herding cattle), Gamila (friend), people at market, Bibi and Baba Zawenna (flour vendors), and Rafiki Kaya (spice vendor).

Tips: Listing the characters on chart paper, in order, will help keep students on track. At the back of the book is a series of Kiswahili phrases; consider teaching students "Hodi," the word spoken when arriving at a neighbor's house, so that it can be incorporated into the end of the play.

Fleming, Denise. *Time to Sleep.* New York: Henry Holt, 1997. unpaged. ISBN 080537624.

Grades: K–2

Summary: Bear tells Snail that winter is on its way. Snail passes on the message to Skunk, who passes it on to Turtle, and so on, until the message gets back to Bear. But by then, Bear has already begun hibernating and must be awakened to receive the message!

Roles Needed: Bear, Snail, Skunk, Turtle, Woodchuck, Ladybug

Tips: Use body shapes (tall, small, wide, skinny, flat) to coach the students into more realistic physical portrayals of the animals.

Thompson, Lauren. *Polar Bear Night.* New York: Scholastic, 2003. unpaged. ISBN 0439495245.

Grades: K–1

Summary: A young polar bear cub wakes up at night. Looking for someone to play with, he wanders the frozen North, but all of his friends are sleeping. After witnessing the aurora borealis, he heads home, where his mother is waiting for him.

Roles Needed: Mother polar bear, polar bear cub, moon, walruses, seals, whales, several stars in the star shower.

Tips: This quiet story was recommended for circle drama by some kindergarten students. Use one student each for the polar bear cub and mother; use multiple casting for the animals, and invite everyone around the circle to create the flickering, bright star shower. Invite the audience to create sound effects that bring the cold, quiet evening to life.

■ WHEN DISRUPTIVE STUDENTS STEAL THE SPOTLIGHT

With drama work, instructors will often have the greatest struggles with the extreme ends of the behavioral spectrum: the extremely disruptive students and those who are reluctant or shy. Both require attention.

Every class has disruptive students, those who call out without raising their hands, call out unflattering comments to fellow students, or try to change the story as they go (often accompanied by audience laughter, which just spurs them on).

Because ground rules have been clearly articulated, students know the expectations for the activity. Usually, what works best is simply to calmly say to the student, "I'm sorry, but that falls outside of our ground rules. Please step out of the scene and sit on the chairs at the back." As the instructor, stay calm. Don't exacerbate the situation by responding with anger or frustration. (Sometimes, that's just what the disruptive student wants; he or she knows it will make *the instructor* look foolish.) No child has the right to "steal" the pantomime by focusing inappropriate attention on himself or herself.

If the child balks, respond with, "I'm sorry you're disappointed. We can talk about it in one/two/five minutes and see if you're ready to come back then." Then flip forward a few pages and stick your finger there to hold your place. Then continue on with the story. When you arrive at the page you marked with your finger, it will be a reminder that it's time to ask the student to rejoin the class. Because he or she will be sitting on a chair where he or she can still see the action, the student is still getting the benefits of observation.

If a disruptive student has been removed from a role and the part has to be recast, do so quickly and quietly. Use words like, "Who would like to be Little Red Riding Hood *while Kim is away*?" This makes it clear that when Kim is ready to return, she will have her part back.

Most children hate to be taken out of the "fun" activity, and most will choose to sit quietly and wait for the opportunity to return to the action. Once a few minutes have passed, ask the student, "Do you think you're ready to come back now?" Make sure he or she understands what to do differently the next time.

■ CREATING A SAFE SPACE FOR RELUCTANT PARTICIPANTS

Reluctant students may be so shy or withdrawn that they do not want to participate at all. Interestingly, many reluctant students are those who are academic achievers who fear failure and the perceived "humiliation" they'll endure if they fumble publicly.

There are several ways to encourage fearful or reluctant students. First, for at least the first three times you do narrative pantomime, cast roles only to those who volunteer for them. Let the shy or withdrawn students observe the process so they cam become comfortable with the patterns and procedures of narrative pantomime. Once they are familiar with the routines, they may feel more secure and ready to participate.

Next, consider a transitional step. When working with sound effects, assign an effect to a group of four or five students instead of to the entire audience. This starts to increase the responsibility of a shy student while maintaining the safety that comes from sitting in the audience.

Another option is multiple casting. Pair a shy student with a gregarious one. For example, in "A Good Night's Sleep," there could be two cats instead of one. Another way to do multiple casting in animal stories is to ask one person to be the front of an animal and the other to be the back. If a shy student is assigned to be the back half of the cow, for example, he can literally bury his head in his partner's back and not have to look at the audience.

Finally, for students from preschool through second grade, being the "book holder" can be a safe but participating role in a play. These students sit or stand, holding the illustrations of the book up so that the group can be reminded of the story's order.

Most children gain confidence from creative drama work, especially in early grades, where the focus remains on improvisation as opposed to performance in front of a formal audience. As student skills improve in retelling stories, they will soon be ready for the Creation Model of narrative pantomime.

■ THE CREATION MODEL: STUDENT-LED NARRATIVE PANTOMIME (GRADES 4 AND ABOVE)

Once students have reached fourth grade, they are generally ready to take over the teacher's role as narrator and even to create their own stories. A group of students might research the historical event of Washington crossing the Delaware and create a narrative. One student reads it while the others act it out. Consider groups of about five students. If possible, aim for groups with odd numbers of students in them, which guarantees that, if a decision comes to a vote, there won't be a stalemate.

This model extends beyond a single visit to the media center. Collaborative planning may make it possible for a story written in the classroom to be brought to life in the media center. Still, because this is not a full-fledged play, in which actors would be responsible for their own lines, the preparation process is much faster.

Whereas the storytime version of narrative pantomime focuses on spontaneous and improvisational work in which the text is explored by students, the Creation Model can be used most effectively as an assessment tool, an end-of-study tool in which students showcase what they have learned. For this reason, students may be likely to ask if they can use props and costumes in their preparations, as students perceive creation pantomime as more of a performance and less of an exploratory activity. Give each group an empty box or crate in which to store supplies as they are brought in. Asking students to bring in these elements in advance ensures that the supplies will be there on the day they are needed. To stop "stuff" from overwhelming the performers, consider limiting the number of props to what will fit in the box.

The students also decide in advance which student will have which role(s) and who will narrate. Usually, students working in small groups do not have any extra students to be the audience, though they could assign one or two students to provide sound effects. They might decide to take turns, with one narrator reading one paragraph and the second narrator reading the next. Student groups who cannot decide this quickly will need the instructor's help in making quick assignments. This step should be quick and not occupy the better part of a class session. One student might be assigned to direct the piece to ensure that volume, voice levels, and interesting body postures are included.

News Reporting

Another approach for student-centered pantomime is to have the narrator assume the role of a news reporter. When television reporters report from the scene, they narrate the events as they unfold behind their back. The same technique can be applied to pantomime. For example, a student-created pantomime about explorers could begin with, "I'm Pete Bradford, speaking to you live from the Spanish court, where Columbus is about to ask King Ferdinand and Queen Isabella to fund his three-ship voyage to the New World." The planning sheet on page 65 can help students organize their thoughts and keep track of deadlines.

Planning Sheet: Student-Created Pantomime

Name _____

Other Students in Group: _____

_____

Topic of Scene _____

Roles in Our Scene:

Role   Played by

_____

_____

_____

_____

_____

--continue on back side of paper if needed--

We will need these props, costumes, and other items:

Item   Will be brought/made by:

_____

_____

_____

_____

_____

--continue on back side of paper if needed--

What do we need to know before we can start planning our project?

Important Dates:

Project Assigned: _____
Show rough version of scene: _____
Show final version of scene: _____

Topics for Creation Model Narrative Pantomime

▶ *Social Studies*

An obvious starting point for students in grades 4 and above is the social studies curriculum, in which historic events can be reenacted. Here are some social studies topics that you can use with your students:

- Reenact Columbus's visit to Spain to ask Queen Isabella and King Ferdinand for their support for his voyage to the New World.

- Assign half the groups the task of showing Columbus's arrival in the New World from the point of view of the explorers. Assign the other half to show Columbus's arrival in the New World from the point of view of the natives.

- For Constitution Day, divide students into groups of six or seven. Ask the students to research the major signatories to the U.S. Constitution. Use Howard Chandler Christy's painting, *Scene at the Signing of the Constitution,* available at http://teachpol.tcnj.edu/amer_pol_hist/fi/0000004e.htm, for inspiration. Ask one student to "narrate" the scene by acting as an on-the-scene news reporter. The reporter will explain who the major figures are and what is transpiring.

- Reenact the signing of the Declaration of Independence. Use the famous painting by Trumbull (http://www.ushistory.org/declaration/trumbull.htm) as an inspiration point.

- During the Iraq War, many media organizations "embedded" reporters with active troops. The reporters lived and traveled with the soldiers. Ask students to imagine they are "embedded" with Harriet Tubman during one of her trips leading slaves to freedom. What obstacles did they encounter?

- Stage a live broadcast from Ford's Theatre on the night of Lincoln's assassination.

- Reenact events from Washington's life: the anecdotal chopping down of the cherry tree, crossing the Delaware, Valley Forge, and assuming the presidency.

- Research and reenact the building of the Transcontinental Railroad, including a live report from the "Golden Spike" event, when the two railroads met.

▶ *Literature: Recalling Important Moments from Chapter Books*

Creation pantomime is a great way to assess student understanding of key moments in chapter book reading and provides an opportunity for the media specialist-as-teacher to reinforce concepts learned in the classroom.

Creation pantomimes about works of literature can be done several times while a book is being read in class. For example, after a long weekend, small groups could be asked to do creation pantomimes summarizing the key points in chapters that have already been read. They can also be made to answer the question, "What is the scene in which [the character] begins to change?" "What is the pivotal scene for the plot?"

Another option is to assign each group a different key event from a novel. Each group performs in sequence, helping students to review all chapters of a novel prior to an end-of-novel test.

Here are some examples of how creation pantomime can interface with literature:

- Replay Karana's "rescue" at the end of Scott O'Dell's *Island of the Blue Dolphins.* Write the events in the students' own words.
- Act out the scene in *Because of Winn-Dixie* in which India Opal meets Winn-Dixie at the grocery store.
- While reading *Tuck Everlasting* in class, the teacher reads the chapter in which Ma Tuck hits the constable with the axe. In the media center, student groups plan and enact pantomimes predicting what will happen to Ma or Winnie next.
- Reenact the moment when the treasure box is found in Louis Sachar's *Holes.*

▶ Science

The science curriculum is often the most overlooked area for drama integration, but kinesthetic-oriented learning can work to reinforce scientific concepts. While these could be done strictly with silent pantomime, the presence of a narrator and script keeps the task focused and clarifies concepts. Potential science topics include

- the life cycle of a seed,
- the life cycle of a butterfly,
- the life cycle of a tree,
- how rain is made,
- how weather fronts function,
- Newton's Laws of Physics (assign each group a different law),
- the stages of a volcano's eruption,
- how cells split, and
- how germs or viruses spread from person to person.

▶ Math

Encourage students to write and then enact story problems.

▶ Creative Writing

Student-created pantomimes also work well to share creative writing projects.

■ BECOMING COMFORTABLE WITH NARRATIVE PANTOMINE THROUGH REPETITION

Narrative pantomime activities improve with practice. Consider blocking out at least three consecutive activities to explore narrative pantomime, with a different story or theme for each visit. As students become more comfortable with the concept, their enthusiasm and commitment will increase. Once the class is familiar with the process of narrative pantomime, the focus shifts from learning the procedures to concentrating on the content.

Both instructors and students benefit from repeated narrative pantomime efforts. Repeating pantomime activities in at least three lessons will build everyone's confidence and connectedness. In addition, instructors gain the ability to see students—especially those who are kinesthetically gifted but might not shine in "typical" library lessons—in a new way.

■ CONCLUSION

I often hear back from parents who can tell me exactly what story we read, who played who, and how a child reenacted the story at home. Sometimes children reenact stories at recess or during choice time. Narrative pantomime embeds itself in children's memories. They remember the experience *and* the content.

Narrative pantomime is a simple and effective way to introduce drama and build student enthusiasm for it. Narrative pantomime is improvisational and "in the moment," focusing more on the story and less on the repetitions that come with drama-for-performance. The teacher-as-storyteller provides the glue that holds the process together and keeps it on track.

■ REFERENCES

Freeman, Judy. 2006. *Books Kids Will Sit Still for 3: A Read-Aloud Guide.* Westport, CT: Libraries Unlimited. 915p. ISBN 159158163X; 1591581648 (pbk.).

Kelner, Lenore Blank, and Rosalind M. Flynn. 2006. *A Dramatic Approach to Reading Comprehension: Strategies and Activities for Classroom Teachers.* Portsmouth, NH: Heinemann. 229pp. ISBN 0325007942 (pbk.).

McMaster, Jennifer Catney. 1998. " 'Doing' Literature: Using Drama to Build Literacy." *The Reading Teacher* 51(7): 574–580.

Spolin, Viola. 1999. *Improvisation for the Theater.* 3d ed. Evanston, IL: Northwestern University Press, 1999. 412pp. ISBN 081014008X (pbk.).

Sun, Ping-Yun. 2003. *Using Drama and Theatre to Promote Literacy Development: Some Basic Classroom Applications.* The Clearinghouse on Reading, English, and Communication Digest no. 187. Available at http://reading.indiana.edu/ieo/digests/d187.html (accessed August 14, 2006).

Some of the techniques in this chapter are adapted from observations of classroom work by Lenore Blank Kelner and Sean Layne.

Chapter 4
Animating History: Biography Wax Museum (Grades 3 and Up)

■ INTRODUCTION

Many tourists are familiar with Madame Tussaud's Wax Museums. These museums contain galleries full of wax mannequins precisely crafted to resemble celebrities, politicians, and historical figures. Visitors marvel over the similarities between the wax figure and the real person.

This student, caught between museum visits, plays George Washington in a Revolutionary War wax museum project.

Creating a school wax museum builds on this concept. Many schools have biography units in which students must prepare "reports" about notable figures from the past and present. Instead of a lengthy written project, why not bring those figures to life by creating a wax museum in which its figures "come alive" and orate biographical information?

The theatrical term for one person making an uninterrupted speech is *monologue*. The prefix "mono" means "one." This chapter focuses on how students can research a historical figure, then craft and perform a biographical monologue in the role of that figure.

This project's primary focus is performance, not improvisation. For this reason, prescripted and prerehearsed text is emphasized here instead of improvised, on-the-spot text. In most cases, the text is memorized, but in some cases the text may be outlined on small index cards. The final presentations are made in front of students from other classrooms who "visit" the museum to see its biographical figures come to life.

This performance setting is a tremendous motivator for participating students, who want to present their very best to their audience. Placing a biography report in a real-world creative situation, with real-world consequences, also gives students the opportunity to fuse their research work with their individual creativity.

To create a wax museum, individual students research the biography of a famous person. They then assume the character of that person, preparing a one- to two-minute speech in the first person. Performing students then create an "on/off" switch for their visitors to use to "activate" the wax figure and dress in clothing that mimics that worn by the notable figure. The media center or other space is arranged to resemble a gallery. Other classes are invited to view the museum by walking through the exhibits. When they find a wax figure that intrigues them, they activate the "on/off" button, and the performing student delivers the memorized brief speech.

On/off buttons can be made from simple household items.

■ STEPS FOR CREATING A WAX MUSEUM

Step One: Working Collaboratively with (a) Classroom Teacher(s), Decide on a Focus for the Wax Museum

One option is to make this project a general biography report, meaning that the focus is on biography as a genre and that students may choose to bring any approved figure to life.

With an open approach such as this one, be cautious about which contemporary figures are permitted for the purposes of online research. Safe resources for biographical information, such as subscription databases or encyclopedias, often concentrate on biographical information for well-known figures of the past, but they tend to miss current TV or music stars. Biographies of current celebrities may be a thorny issue. Some of children's most intriguing celebrities cannot be found in books or in vetted online research tools. Especially with elementary students, the instructor may wish to have some control over the resources a student can use and discourage students from randomly Googling (at school or home) or accessing Wikipedia, with its lengthy articles, high reading level, and always-being-edited status. One alternative to this is to limit student selection to the items in the print biography collection or to say, "When we go into the computer lab this morning, you will have 10 minutes to browse in *World Book Encyclopedia Online/Grolier Online.* You may choose any figure you can find there."

Another option ties into the social studies or history curriculum. In this second example, the media specialist and classroom teacher(s) select a particular historical theme or era, prepare a list of notable persons from that era, and invite students to select a person from that list to bring to life. Possibilities for this approach include

- world explorers,
- inventors and/or famous scientists,
- U.S. presidents or first ladies,
- people of the Revolutionary War,
- notable figures of the Civil War or abolition movement,
- leaders of the civil rights movement,
- notable figures of World War I,
- notable figures of World War II,
- notable figures by decade, and
- heroes. (To steer younger students away from inappropriate content, consider structuring the assignment so that the wax museum speech includes an explanation of why the figure deserves to be called a hero.)

Clustering biographies together so that they have a connecting theme or era can enhance classroom learning, as students will be able to connect what they have learned from the study of their individual with a broader historical or thematic context.

Step Two: Prepare the Evaluation Rubric

For a formal, planned presentation like the wax museum, it is extremely effective to distribute the evaluation rubric to upper elementary students at the same time that the project is introduced. Students have a better sense of the overall expectations and are more likely to check the rubric before asking a question. This makes them more confident and independent and, because less instructor time is spent answering rudimentary questions, more time can be spent working with students with greater needs. A rubric can also be developed as part of Step Three (below), with student input. See the sample rubric on page 73.

As a planning tool, a rubric helps collaborating partners clarify expectations and prepare a "unified front" for students. It gives everyone a common checklist, avoiding potential communication failures.

Step Three: Introduce the Project to Your Students

If this project is planned in a flexibly scheduled environment, it may be possible to present this in conjunction with the collaborating classroom teacher(s). If not, decide which instructor will make the introduction. Be sure to include deadlines. Talk through the rubric and answer any questions. If doing a themed approach to the biographies, distribute the list of approved personalities and give students a few moments to choose two or three favorites. Then call on students randomly and let them choose a topic, first-come, first-served.

Step Four: Research

Using established research protocols and methods, have students conduct and collect research, just as they would for a written project. While working with students, continue to remind them of the *context* for their research: that their research is meant to entertain their visitors. Say, "I see you've marked that so-and-so had seven children, and you've written down all of their names. Do you think their names are important enough to include in his two-minute biography, which is really about his work as a World War II Airborne soldier?"

Step Five: Writing

Now that research has been gathered, students should write their brief speeches using the district's recommended writing process. Ideally, because of their brevity, the speeches will be memorized, but small note cards with bullet points are another option, especially for students with learning disabilities. Avoid having students hold full-sized sheets of paper, as they impair movement. Index cards are preferable because they can be held in the palm of one hand.

If this project doubles as a writing assignment, the classroom teacher may ask for the speech to be turned in for evaluation prior to the continuation of the project.

Step Six: Planning the Wax Museum

Students now move to the planning stages for the wax museum.

Sign. Have each student create a sign identifying himself or herself and the historical figure, for example, "Joe Smith as Paul Revere." This helps to orient visitors to the wax museum.

Wax Museum Rubric

Name _____

	Outstanding	Very Good	Fair	Needs Improvement
Memorization	**4 points** Presentation is completely memorized	**3 points** Presentation is mostly memorized.	**2 points** Presentation is partly memorized.	**1 point** Presentation is not memorized.
Length	**4 points** Presentation runs 1 - 2 minutes.	**3 points** Presentation is a little bit shorter than a minute.	**2 points** Presentation is a lot shorter than a minute.	**1 point** Presentation is way too short.
Introduction	**4 points** Presentation includes who you are and what your person's role was in the Revolutionary War	**3 points** Presentation may be missing who you are or what that person's role was	**2 points** Presentation is missing information.	**1 point** You forgot to mention your person's name and role in the War.
Historical and Interesting Facts	**4 points** The most important facts about your person's life are included. A few lesser-known interesting facts are included	**3 points** Some important facts are included, and there are some interesting facts.	**2 points** Some important information is missing, and some non-important facts are included.	**1 point** A lot of important or interesting information is missing.
Costume	**4 points** Your costume is creative and helps show the audience who your person is	**3 points** Your costume is good.	**2 points** Your costume is limited and makes it hard for people to know something about your person	**1 point** No costume.
Research Process/Effort	**4 points** You used your time well in the computer lab and made a strong effort	**3 points** You usually used your time well in the computer lab and usually made a strong effort	**2 points** You sometimes used your time well in the computer lab and sometimes made a strong effort	**1 point** You did not use your time well and did not make a good effort.
Button and Sign	**4 points** You have a creative on/off button and an easy-to-read sign that includes your name and the name of your character	**3 points** Your button and sign are mostly neatly done and generally easy to read.	**2 points** Your button and sign are sloppily done or parts are missing.	**1 point** No sign or button.

FINAL GRADE: _____ / 28 points = _____ %

COMMENTS:

A sign identifying the actor and the historical figure.

The on/off button or switch. One task, which can be done at home or at school, is to create an "on/off" button or switch. Visitors to a student's exhibit will have to engage this button or switch in order to activate the presentation. Let children come up with this idea on their own as much as possible—it leads to the most innovation and greatest variety. Spray can lids, cosmetic containers, light switches, bottle caps, small boxes, margarine containers, and frozen juice cans can all be transformed. If this activity is to be done in school, ask the food service staff if they have extra bottle caps, cans, foam trays, or containers that students could use to create a button.

Costumes. Students should also be thinking about costuming themselves. During their research, they should find a photograph or image to use as inspiration. Students in many communities will have items at home to use as well as parents who can help assemble the costume.

**A barn jacket, belt slung over the shoulder, and athletic pants
with stripes up the sides create the impression of a war-weary soldier.**

If students have limited resources at home, or if there is time to incorporate this creative process into the curriculum, work on costumes during school hours. Consider beginning a costume box with a few thrift-store button-down shirts, simple skirts, aprons, capes, and caps. Many thrift shop blazers for women have military colors like red or blue and even come with bright gold buttons.

An even simpler—and more creative—approach is to make fabric squares, which can have a variety of uses. I first saw this idea in action when I saw a performance in the late 1980s by the bilingual Pregones theatre company. They used large fabric squares to enhance their costumes and even create prop pieces.

**Lace worn around the shoulders is a quick and easy
way to establish a historical setting.**

To start, visit fabric stores, which often have tables of fabric marked down to $1 or $2 a yard. Try nonstretch fabrics like calico or twill for durability. Decorating fabrics used for upholstery or curtains are too thick to drape nicely. For greatest versatility, choose neutral, classic colors like red, navy, black, tan, and brown. Avoid wild patterns.

Cut the fabric pieces into squares. Fabric comes in various widths, generally 45, 54, or 60 inches. Cut those pieces into 45-, 54-, or 60-inch squares. Seal the ends using a serger or fold the ends over and make a simple seam. Fabric stores sell no-sew, iron-on adhesive hem tape. Trimming edges with pinking shears will also limit raveling.

These fabric squares are very useful for performances. They can be folded in half crosswise into a triangular shape that can be used for an apron, a babushka, an arm sling, or a shawl. Left as a square, the two top corners can be pinned around the neck to make a cape. The fabric can be rolled up to become a baby bundle or a bundle carried by a slave escaping via the Underground Railroad. Draping a fabric swatch over a chair transforms it into a throne; draping it over a table can transform it into Lewis and Clark's tent.

Props. Military hats can be made from folded newspaper, and military swords can be made by rolling up a few sheets of newspaper. Other props can be cut from cardboard boxes and painted with acrylic craft paint. Many students enjoy decorating their desks with items that are associated with the historical figure. For example, in the photo on page 74, Phillis Wheatley holds a feather pen and is writing, which shows the audience the importance of authorship in her career. In the following photo, the student portraying Paul Revere was inspired by Revere's famous self-portrait and arranged his desk with a pitcher and silverware to mirror the items in the painting. As in tourist wax museums, props can help to contextualize the figure. Props are an optional addition to a student's wax museum.

Props help create the world in which the figure lived.

Step Seven: Inviting the Audience

Wax museums are fun when students from other classes come to see them. If the school has a large media center, students can spread out. Wax museums can also be set up in hallways, classrooms, the multipurpose room, or the playground! Allow about 20 minutes for groups to travel through the museum, and put a five-minute break between each one so the performers can let out nervous energy, take a restroom break, get a drink of water, or stretch their legs. If collaborating with more than one class, one class could take the morning shift and another take an afternoon shift in order not to tire out the student performers. In the teacher's lounge, post an invitation to teachers as well as a sign-up sheet. If there is additional time in the curriculum, invite the student performers to create promotional posters to place around the school, perhaps in the style of that historical period.

Step Eight: Setting Up and Final Rehearsals

The day of the wax museum performance, set up the museum space by rearranging tables and chairs so there is adequate traffic flow around them. Avoid a formal traffic pattern—it will exhaust the students at the beginning of the "line," and students whose presentations are at the end of the "line" will get little exposure.

If the wax museum will have several rounds of visitors, student presenters may wish to sit down behind a table or desk instead of standing. Having a table or desk also provides a sense of security. Place the on/off button on the table where visitors can reach it. Tape the sign to the front of the table. If some students are hesitant about memorization, allow them to keep their cards on the table.

Students may stand or sit while performing in the wax museum.

When all of the students have set up their "exhibits," gather the class together for the Welcoming Ritual and a few vocal warm-ups from chapter 2. Then rehearse by having half the class walk around, activating their classmates' buttons and hearing their speeches. Then swap. This helps students have a realistic sense of what to anticipate. Save time for a last-minute restroom and water break, and it's show time!

Step Nine: Wax Museum Open for Business!

While classes come in and out, walk through with a clipboard and observe the student performers while they interact with the visitors. Stand back so as not to intimidate the performers; fill in the rubrics.

Step Ten: Reflection

When the museum has said farewell to its last visitors, hold a feedback session with students.

■ CONCLUSION

A wax museum is a fun and easy way to transform a traditional biography book report into a performance experience that can be shared and enjoyed throughout the school community. Because of its kinesthetic and creative elements, it motivates student researchers to do their best.

By bringing a historical figure to life, students can feel a greater connection to that person and his or her historical period. Here, a student plays Ben Franklin.

Chapter 5
Ideas in Action: Drama Machines (Grades 3 and Up)

▥ INTRODUCTION

This chapter and the next focus on student-created improvisations. The techniques may be based on a story or research project, but they do not ask students to recall or re-create the story, nor do they ask students to prepare a speech. Instead, drama machines ask students to manipulate text into a new product. Students examine a story or a body of research and from it, cull important themes, facts, and lessons. They synthesize this harvested information and demonstrate their understanding through drama machines (this chapter) or tableaus (following chapter). They require higher-level thinking and are deeply satisfying to create and to witness.

A drama machine is an improvised, moving sculpture that captures the essential feelings, elements, or facts about a subject. The teacher begins with an empty playing space and assigns a topic. Students enter the playing space one at a time. Each student contributes a repeated motion along with a sound or phrase, with each new student finding a way to add himself or herself into the existing group. The result is a moving, vocal sculpture with intertwining parts. Drama machines can be done with the entire class or can be performed by small groups.

▥ WARM-UP ACTIVITIES

As with all of the drama techniques discussed in this book, drama machines work best when prefaced by a Welcoming Ritual and drama warm-ups (see chapter 2). The drama warm-up "Make Me a . . ." and its variations are particularly well-suited for drama machines because they focus on manipulating the body to create an image.

■ MODELING THE DRAMA MACHINE TECHNIQUE

Once the opening activities are concluded, it is time to model how drama machines work. There are many approaches to creating a drama machine, but this initial exercise is useful for all approaches. Modeling with a concrete example is the best starting point, although the main lesson drama machine may extend into metaphoric, thematic, or abstract thought. For the modeling, choose a piece of actual machinery with several moving parts that integrate into a whole. The workings of a clock or the motor of a car are examples that will be familiar to students. A favorite modeling example is to ask students to create a washing machine. Here is what this might look like in the media center. The media specialist says,

> Class, today we are going to use our bodies and our voices to make a washing machine. Each member of the group will represent one part of the washing machine. In a machine, each piece is connected to another piece. Each member will contribute a motion and a sound that will help us know what part they are. One member will enter one at a time, positioning themselves around the other members so that by the end, we have a working washing machine. This technique is called a drama machine. John, would you start?

John enters the playing space. He stands straight up with his arms to his sides, then gently turns his shoulders from side to side, making a "whish, whish" noise. He is the agitator.

Mary voluntarily enters the space next. Standing behind John, she tilts her head to the side over and over, making a "buzz" sound. She is the timer at the top of the machine.

When Omar and Savannah both start to enter the playing space at the same time, Omar steps back to allow Savannah to enter next. (If one student does not bow out, the instructor makes a choice about which person should enter the scene next.) Savannah's body becomes limp, and she twirls slowly around John, saying, "Shlump, shlump." She represents an item of clothing in the washer.

Now Omar enters the playing area, standing to John's side, bending up and down from the waist. "Slam!" he says, portraying the lid of the washer. As the students repeat their actions over and over, they subtly alter their personal rhythms, taking turns with their sounds until a pleasing effect is achieved and the teacher brings the machine to a halt.

Instructionally, what has happened? Each student was able to stretch his or her imagination to find something unique to add to the washing machine effect. Each student deconstructed the washer into its separate parts and thought creatively about how to join the group without overshadowing or disrupting the performance of the others.

The modeling takes five to ten minutes and is easy to complete because the students use their prior knowledge of the washing machine.

■ TOOLS FOR BUILDING DRAMA MACHINES: SPACE, ENERGY, AND TIME

Dance educators often use SET (*S*pace, *E*nergy, and *T*ime) to help students add dynamism to their performance. Briefly explain these terms to your students, and they will become a quick and easy shorthand to improve student performance during the improvisations.

Space is how the body fills the area around it. Encourage students to seek out different body levels: high, medium, and low. In the washing machine example, the agitator and the dial have high bodies, the clothes in the machine are in the middle of the visual picture, and the clothes in the washing machine might be portrayed by crouching down low. This adds visual interest and allows observers to see more of the participants in action.

Energy is the way the body moves through space. Is it sharp, like the washing machine's banging lid, or fluid, like the clothes in the machine?

Time is the speed at which the body moves. The agitator in the washing machine moves faster than the clothing, and the dial may move slower than the lid.

Part of what makes a drama machine interesting to watch is that its individual participants use different SETs. This creates intriguing tensions that make the audience want to engage more closely with the participants.

■ SIMPLE DRAMA MACHINE EXERCISES TO USE WITH CONCRETE IMAGES

To introduce students to the drama machine technique, working with concrete examples—replicating actual objects—is most successful. Younger students with limited abstraction abilities need a concrete example in order to be successful. Following a read-aloud, students could be asked to use their bodies to re-create an object from the story, making a drama machine a substitute for narrative pantomime or circle drama. Find a story in which a mechanical object with moving parts is featured (see the list of recommendations at the end of this section).

As an example, consider P. D. Eastman's *Are You My Mother?*, in which a baby bird mistakes several animals, vehicles, and objects for his mother. After reading this story, students might be asked to create the "Snort," the mighty steam shovel that at first intimidates the baby bird but later returns it safely to its nest, where its mother is waiting. Or consider the classic *Mike Mulligan and the Steam Shovel*, by Virginia Lee Burton. After either story, children might create a drama machine in which

- one child is the driver of the Snort, making a "vroom!" sound;
- one scoops his hands up and down to be the bucket, saying, "Clunk! Scoop. Clunk! Scoop";
- one child is the whistle, saying, "SNORT!"; and
- some children are the treads, saying, "Crrrrrr-eak! Crrrrr-eak! Crrrrr-eak!"

Following the story, model the drama machine technique as described above. Then divide the class up into groups of four to five. Say,

> You are going to work with your group to create a drama machine of a _____. A drama machine is like a moving sculpture that makes noises. One student begins the drama machine by creating a gesture—or movement—and adding a sound that goes with it, like in the washing machine example we did together. She repeats the movement and gesture over and over until the second person enters the scene. The second student's body should connect with the first student's body so it is clear they are part of the same object. He adds his own repeating movement and gesture. Then the third person comes in, connects to one of the other students, and adds a repeating movement and sound.

While it is tempting to list all of the elements that could be used in a drama machine by saying, "We're making a car. That means someone is the engine, and someone will make the wheels," allow the children to come up with their own roles and sounds. The results are far more interesting that way, and students engage in higher-level thinking.

Allow three to five minutes for the groups to prepare, giving occasional timing updates so students know how long they have to keep working. For example, say,

> You have one more minute. If you haven't done your machine one time through yet, you should do that now.

It's important to reflect on the concept of time. Spontaneous and creative ideas often kick in when students sense a deadline, and a time limit also prevents endless debate. The media specialist should give concrete time deadlines and could even wear a stopwatch to "look serious" about time. However, the actual time of an activity should be judged according to how the students are working. If each group seems to complete the task before the allocated time limit, the media specialist can call, "Time's up!" early. If the time deadline comes and everyone is actively working and engaged, the media specialist can let the preparations run longer. In any event, it is important to give time reminders; it helps students stay on track.

When the time is up, ask each group to come and sit in a circle. Remind them of what is expected of them as audience members while others are performing:

> 1. Keep voices quiet so everyone can hear what is being said.
> 2. Focus your eyes on the performers.
> 3. Keep your hands in your lap.
> 4. Laugh at the funny parts.
> 5. Clap at the end to show that you appreciate their effort.

Let each group step into the center of the circle to show off their work. Allow the observers to applaud briefly after each "performance." Applause is a way of showing appreciation for a job well done.

Feedback

After each group's performance, spend a few moments gathering feedback. Feedback is an opportunity for the audience to tell the performers what they observed. Feedback helps performers understand the impact of their work on others. Structure feedback using the "sandwich" technique, in which constructive criticism is "sandwiched" between positive comments. This helps keep morale high. Structure student feedback into three clear sections:

1. **Positive feedback.** Start by asking, "What did the group do well?"

2. **Constructive criticism.** The goal of constructive criticism is not to belittle a performer but to offer suggestions that, if adopted, could help the performers improve their next presentation. Try a comment such as, "If the group were to perform this again, what would make this performance better?" Note this positive tone, which is preferable to a negative comment like, "What was not very good about this performance?"

3. **Strong parts to keep in the next performance.** Complete the "sandwich" with a positive comment: "What was so good that is should *not* be changed?" This question is especially important for young performers, whose self-evaluation techniques may not yet be fully developed. They need this reinforcement, or they may change *everything* when repeating the activity.

Revision

Tell the students that they are going to work with their groups again. They should think about their sandwich feedback and think about how they can use their colleagues' advice to improve their project.

In addition, they are going to concentrate on their voices. The first time they showed the class their presentations, they concentrated on the *body* (creating an interesting motion) and on the *imagination* (creating an interesting word or sound). Now they are going to make the *voice* as interesting as possible. Ask them to think about how they might use these vocal skills to make their performance more meaningful. (Posting these questions is a good reinforcer as well.)

- **Volume.** Would your performance improve if it were louder? Softer?

- **Speed.** Would your performance improve if it were faster? Slower?

- **Pitch.** Would your performance improve if it were higher? Lower?

- **Tone/Energy.** Would your performance improve if your voice was smooth? Sharp? Peaceful? Scared? Crying?

Demonstrate each example for the students using the sentence, "I think it will rain" so students can see how vocal choices can affect and improve their performance. Then give the groups a few minutes to revise their work before they demonstrate their work to the class again.

Assessment

Many drama machines are ungraded, exploratory activities. However, it is useful to be aware of how skills are developing. The chapter 3 running record (page 39) can assist with assessment. In addition, this activity can be quickly assessed using the drama machine assessment rubric (page 87).

Assessment Rubric: Drama Machines

Name _____

Class _____

Key:

+   Exceeded expectations
✓   Met expectations
-         Did not meet expectations

Did you . . .	Self Evaluation	Teacher Evaluation
Use your body to connect with other students in your Machine?		
Create a Drama Machine that represented the object successfully?		
Use your voice in an interesting way? Could others hear it?		
Cooperate with your team?		
Concentrate and focus on what you were doing?		
Use classroom feedback to improve the second performance?		

Books That Work Well with This Technique

McMullan, Kate, and Jim McMullan. *I Stink!* New York: Joanna Cotler, 2002. unpaged. ISBN 0060298499.

A garbage truck's view of the world is funny for listeners and told with a bold and exuberant voice. Groups create machines demonstrating the various mechanical workings of the truck.

Dahl, Roald. *Charlie and the Chocolate Factory.* New York: Knopf, 1964. 161pp. ISBN 0394810112.

A magical factory of pipes, elevators, and machines awaits children who possess a lucky Golden Ticket. Brainstorm the various rooms and machines that, one by one, transform visitors to Wonka's factory, and sequence them on a white board. Assign each group one of those machines to create.

Joyce, William. *Santa Calls.* New York: HarperCollins, 1993. unpaged. ISBN 0060211342 (lib. bdg.).

Brainstorm a list of wacky machines in the book. Each group chooses one and creates a drama machine for it.

Kalman, Maira. *Fireboat: The Heroic Adventures of the* John J. Harvey. New York: Putnam, 2002. unpaged. ISBN 0399239537.

Each person in the group demonstrates one fact about how the fireboat worked.

Lister, Mary. *The Winter King and the Summer Queen.* Ill. Diana Mayo. Cambridge, MA: Barefoot Books, 2002. unpaged. ISBN 1841483575.

The Summer Queen rules over the Land of the Flaming Sun, and the Winter King leads the Land of Icy Darkness. The royals agree to share the earth, with each kingdom reigning over six months of the year. Divide the class into two large groups. If the class is balanced in terms of gender, consider asking the girls to represent the Summer Queen's Land of the Flaming Sun and the boys to represent the King's Land of Icy Darkness. Ask each group to create a drama machine that communicates the five senses (touch, smell, sight, sound, and taste) of that kingdom. Post the five senses on the board to help students brainstorm. Because this is a larger group activity, allow approximately 10 minutes for preparations.

■ DRAMA MACHINES AND LITERATURE

Drama machines can be used in more meaningful ways, asking students to stretch toward more abstract thinking. For example, drama machines can be used to explore characters in literature. In this sense, they are a living mind map or graphic organizer, with each student contributing another fact about the character.

This use of drama machines requires higher-level thinking. Instead of re-creating an object already seen in a book, students must choose what information to include and create a new product. This activity is recommended for grades 3 and up.

Sample Lesson

Consider this example:

> A third grade class comes to the media center to participate in story time and an activity about Rachel Vail's picture book *Sometimes I'm Bombaloo* (2002). In this book, the main character Katie confesses that while she is usually a nice girl. However, when she becomes angry, she transforms into an evil twin called "Bombaloo." The book shows how children can sometimes exhibit two very different personalities: the sweet Katie and the angry Bombaloo.
>
> The media specialist would like children to show their understanding for these two halves of the child's personality by having the students create drama machines.
>
> After leading volunteers in a modeling example, such as the washing machine exercise earlier in the chapter, the media specialist reads and discusses the story aloud. The students participate in a handful of warm-up exercises. Then, the media specialist divides the class into small groups of four or five students. She asks each group to create a drama machine that will describe the "Bombaloo" character to the audience, saying,
>
>> You are not going to make a statue of the actual "Bombaloo" person, with arms and feet and legs and a head. Instead, you're going to create a sculpture that will give us the *feeling* of the character. Your goal is a moving sculpture that answers the question, "What is Bombaloo like?" Each person will choose a word or phrase *and* an action to contribute to the sculpture.

The media specialist distributes an organizing/planning worksheet (page 90) and says, "This worksheet will help your group brainstorm, choose the best ideas, and organize yourselves into an interesting drama machine. You have 10 minutes to work. Good luck!"

Planning Sheet:
Literature Drama Machine

Group Members:

_____

_____

_____

Directions:
Brainstorm words or phrases that describe the topic and write them in the center of the graphic organizer. Then let each person in the group pick a word or phrase and create a movement that goes with it.

Hints for choosing a word or phrase:
A word can:

be an adjective, like "beautiful" or "fierce."
be a verb, like, "jumping" or "swooping."
be an adverb, like, "softly" or "quickly."

A phrase can:

be in the voice of the topic: "I'm so sorry."
describe the feeling of the topic: "Sad, sad, sad."
describe the topic in a simile: "as tiny as a toothpick."
describe the topic with a metaphor: "a rock of a man."

Hints for creating a great Drama Machine:
Have one person enter at a time.
Repeat your action and word/phrase over and over. Create an interesting rhythm.
When you enter the playing space, connect to someone who is already there.
Use *Space, Energy, and Time* to create interesting body shapes.
Use *Pitch, Volume, Speed, and Tone/Energy* to create interesting voices.

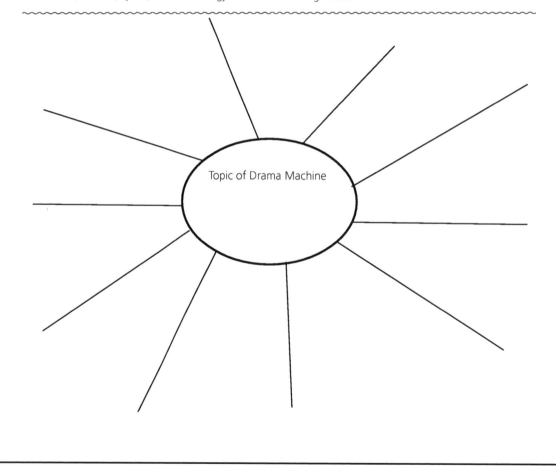

Topic of Drama Machine

When the students fill it out, it resembles this:

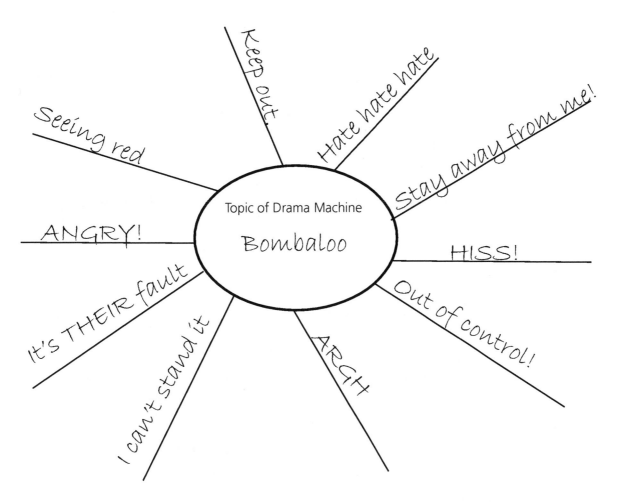

Completing the worksheet has many purposes. Notice that the graphic organizer has more empty slots than there are students in the group. This encourages students to delve deeply into the character and to think of a variety of ways in which a character's personality can be expressed. It also gives all students a choice of which word or phrase to choose, as there will be some unclaimed words or phrases. No one is stuck with the "leftover" topic. It also helps to scaffold and structure the groups' discussions. It can also be collected by the instructors and used as an informal assessment of understanding.

When roles are chosen, students decide on an order to enter the playing space. Each selects a repetitive movement to accompany his or her text. As they rehearse, students will find natural rhythmic give-and-take as they speak with one another.

Students may need instructor assistance in connecting their bodies with one another. Remind students that all machines have parts that connect and touch. In a car, for example, gears interface with each other, a car wheel is connected to its axle, and the windshield wiper is attached to the base of the windshield. Connectedness is what makes a drama machine look like a single sculpture, not four or five individuals.

When time is up, students gather in a circle. One at a time, groups enter the circle and use it as their playing space. After reflection and "sandwich" feedback, groups rehearse again, then give their final presentations.

They are evaluated according to the assessment sheet on page 87, which is completed by both instructor and student.

Imagine the angry drama machine students might create as they utter frustrated comments like, "I hate this!" or, "I can't stand my brother!" These verbal examples clearly demonstrate that students understand who "Bombaloo" is.

Alternate lesson: Assign half the groups to create "Bombaloo" and half to create Katie.

Extension

To extend this activity, ask the same groups to create a second machine that shows what Katie is like when she is herself. Finally, ask the groups to find a way to transition from "Katie" to "Bombaloo." (For tips on coaching students on making the transition, refer to chapter 2's "Make Me a . . ." extension.) The final product begins with each student joining the machine, establishing "Bombaloo," then the students shifting their bodies until they form the "Katie" machine. This extension allows the students to explore the sometimes difficult concept of duality of character: the idea that the same person can sometimes behave in two disparate ways.

Literary Objectives to Explore with Drama Machines

Other possibilities for using drama machines to explore literature include the following:

- **Setting.** For Tomie dePaola's *Legend of the Bluebonnet* (1983), ask students to brainstorm the desert setting. What sounds (like crackling dry ground) or words like ("hot" or "dry") can they use to bring the setting to life? (This is adapted from the author's observation of Lenore Blank Kelner's Environment Orchestra lesson.)

- **Point of view: Picture book.** For Kevin Henkes's *Lilly's Purple Plastic Purse* (1996), ask half of the groups to make a Lilly drama machine and the other half to make one for her teacher, Mr. Slinger. Each machine should show the moment at which Lilly's purse is taken away, and each student should contribute a word or phrase that shows what the character is thinking. For example, Lilly's machine might have a student who says, "He isn't fair!", whereas Mr. Slinger's machine might say, "I need Lilly to pay attention right now."

- **Point of view: Chapter book.** In the middle grade book *Jacob's Rescue*, by Malka Drucker and Michael Halperin (1993), the Jewish boy Jacob is hidden by a Christian family in Warsaw during the Holocaust. In one high-tension scene, a soldier searches the family's apartment while Jacob hides under the sink. Create a different drama machine for each person in the scene.

- **Character growth and change: Chapter book.** In Scott O'Dell's Newbery Award-winning novel *Island of the Blue Dolphins* (1960), Karana gradually becomes more independent and self-sufficient. As a class, brainstorm key moments in the book that demonstrate her level of independence (i.e., running off the boat to rescue her brother, her attempted escape from the island in a handmade canoe, making her own home with lamps; befriending an island dog; and greeting her "rescuers"). Assign a different episode to each group to create a drama machine that shows how Karana perceives herself at that point in the book.

- **Conflict: Picture book.** In Pamela Duncan Edwards's *Gigi and Lulu's Gigantic Fight* (2002), illustrated by Henry Cole, the two best friends have an argument. Ask half the groups to represent Gigi and half to represent Lulu. Each group should make two machines: one explaining why they are best friends with the other, and one showing why they are fighting. If time allows, have students transition between the two.

■ DRAMA MACHINES AND HISTORY RESEARCH

A drama machine can also help build and assess students' understanding of a research topic. Imagine this example in the media center:

> A middle grade class has been researching the causes of the Civil War as part of a collaborative lesson between the Media Specialist and the classroom teacher. After a Welcoming Ritual, warm-ups, and a modeling Drama Machine exercise, the instructors divide the class in half: one representing the North and the other, the South. Each half is asked to create a Drama Machine that illustrates their side's reasons for going to war. The classroom teacher says,
>
> > For this exercise, each person must create a unique word phrase and action. The same graphic organizer used in the earlier exercise can help you brainstorm with your classmates.
>
> As the students break into groups, the instructors notice that quickly, a student in each group claims "slavery" as their contribution to the group. The groups then sputter and stall a bit. Then the students race back to their research and textbooks in search of other, less obvious, reasons for going to war.
>
> After a few frenzied moments of practice and preparation, each group shares its result with the class, followed by feedback, revision, final performances, and assessment as described in earlier sections of this chapter.

Notice how the students were forced to return to their research and look beyond the surface answers in order to make this activity a success. By forcing each student to contribute a different idea, a greater scope of reasons was discovered and expressed. This deepened the students' understanding and perspective. The students enjoyed the spontaneous "play," but were able to do so only when they were fueled with the research.

Topics for History Drama Machines

Other possibilities for drama machines and history include the following:

- **Biography of explorers.** Assign each group a different world explorer. After researching the life and travels of an explorer, create a drama machine that tells the audience about his or her major goals and accomplishments.
- **Trail of Tears.** Create drama machines showing the perspectives of Native Americans and U.S. government officials.
- **Controversial contemporary issues.** Instead of preparing formal papers, ask one student group to perform a "pro" drama machine and another to perform a "con."

■ DRAMA MACHINES AND CONCEPTS: A PERFORMANCE PROJECT WITH THE WHOLE CLASS

Drama machines can also be used to explore concepts and to share the findings in a formal performance. Imagine this example, a collaboration between the media specialist and the building's music teacher:

A fourth-grade class in metropolitan Detroit is researching the history and culture of the early twentieth century. In small research groups, they are in the process of exploring a variety of social and historical topics from which they will write original sketches and vignettes that will culminate in a public performance. To tie their historical studies to the students' hometown legacy, the automotive industry, the music teacher and media specialist wish to introduce the concept of Henry Ford's assembly line and bring it to life using historical photographs as source material.

The media specialist prepares a PowerPoint™ featuring period photographs of assembly lines as well as images of Diego Rivera's famous Detroit Industry murals, located in the Detroit Institute of Arts, a museum familiar to the students. The images are enlarged using a data projector, which allows students to see the details of the images.

The media specialist asks students to describe what they see in the images. Students brainstorm words that described what assembly lines did, what they produced, why they were useful, and how it might feel to be an assembly line worker. The media specialist records their observations onto a white board: "All in a row," "Make it the same," "Repeat," "Building cars," "I do one part," "Again," and more.

The media specialist, music teacher, and students discuss and select their favorite phrases. The music teacher points out that each word phrase can be set to a musical rhythm, as shown in the following example.

Beat 1	Beat 2	Beat 3	Beat 4
All	in	a	row.
Do one part!	(silent)	Do one part!	(silent)
Make it	the same.	Make it	the same.
Re-peat!	Re-peat!	Re-peat!	Re-peat!
Ag--ain.			
Buil-	ding	carrrrrr--------------------s.	

The instructors divide the class into smaller groups of four to five students each, giving each group a word phrase or rhythmic pattern. Each group devises a repetitive gesture to accompany the phrase.

After a few minutes of rehearsal, the groups line up to represent the long, linear assembly line. (In this case, a flat, two-dimensional stage picture is preferable to an intertwined sculpture because it emphasizes the long assembly line.)

The music teacher stands before the assembly line as "conductor," using musical hand gestures as if conducting a choir ("come in," "cut off," "crescendro/get louder," and "decrescendo/get softer"). She instructs the students that when she points to their group, they should perform their text and gestures over and over until she cues them to stop or change.

She then begins conducting the impromptu assembly line. Each group has an opportunity to "solo" their phrases. Then she cues other groups to join, layering their sounds and motions on top of the other group. For example, "Re-peat! Re-peat! Re-peat! Re-peat!" is said simultaneously with "Againnnnnnnnnnnnn," creating an instant musical composition.

At its climax, the students' voices are loud and percussive, finally ending in a sudden silence.

The process takes one class period and is followed up by several refining rehearsals led solely by the music teacher.

Using photographs to tap into their visual literacy and using the skills of voice, body, imagination, concentration, and cooperation, the students mastered the concept of the assembly line. They know from experience about the tedium of repetition, the cacophony of sounds, and the number of people required to make the assembly line work.

Topics to Use with This Technique

This is one of the most challenging models because it involves synchronizing the actions of several groups into a harmonious whole. However, it is a great addition to a school concert or musical as a way of illustrating a concept or a process. Options for this technique include the following:

- **Barn-raising.** After brainstorming the steps used by the Amish to put up a barn, assign one step to each group. Each group then performs in order.
- **Metamorphosis.** Assign each group a different phase of the caterpillar-to-butterfly metamorphosis.
- **Water cycle.** What are the properties of water? Vapor? Rain? Assign each phase to a group, whose drama machine should show the physical qualities and use words to describe those qualities.

■ CONCLUSION

Drama machines are one of the many techniques that encourage students to think deeply and do excellent academic work while having fun, tapping into different learning modalities, demonstrating personal talents, and working collaboratively. Drama machines can be executed in as few as 15 minutes, making them a time-efficient way to explore content and assess learning.

■ REFERENCES

Burton, Virginia Lee. 1999 (c1939). *Mike Mulligan and his Steam Shovel.* 60th anniv. ed. Boston: Houghton Mifflin. 44pp. ISBN 0395169615.

dePaola, Tomie. 1983. *The Legend of the Bluebonnet: An Old Tale of Texas.* New York: Putnam. 30pp. ISBN 0399209379; 0399209387 (pbk.).

Drucker, Malka, and Michael Halperin. 1993. *Jacob's Rescue: A Holocaust Story.* New York: Bantam Skylark. 117pp. ISBN 0553089765.

Eastman, P. D. 1960. *Are You My Mother?* New York: Random House. unpaged. ISBN 0679890475.

Edwards, Pamela Duncan. 2002. *Gigi and Lulu's Gigantic Fight.* New York: Katherine Tegen Books. unpaged. ISBN 0060507535.

Fontichiaro, Kristin. 2006. "Drama Machines: Learning Alive!" *School Library Media Activities Monthly* 22(6) (February): 29–31.

Henkes, Kevin. 1996. *Lilly's Purple Plastic Purse.* New York: Greenwillow. unpaged. ISBN 068812898X (lib. bdg.).

Lister, Mary. 2002. *The Winter King and the Summer Queen.* Illustrated by Diana Mayo. Cambridge, MA: Barefoot Books. unpaged. ISBN 1841483575.

O'Dell, Scott. 1990 (c1960). *Island of the Blue Dolphins.* Boston: Houghton Mifflin. 181pp. ISBN 039553680.

Rivera, Diego. 1932–1933. *Detroit Industry.* Fresco. (Detroit Institute of Arts). Available at http://www.dia.org/collections/AmericanArt/33.10.html (accessed January 15, 2007).

Thomas, Mark. n.d. *American Business History: Images.* Available at http://faculty.virginia.edu/hius341/images (accessed January 15, 2007).

Vail, Rachel. 2002. *Sometimes I'm Bombaloo.* New York: Scholastic. unpaged. ISBN 0439087554.

Walter P. Reuther Library, Wayne State University. n.d. *The Faces of Detroit.* Available at http://www.reuther.wayne.edu/faces/assemblyline.html. (accessed January 15, 2007).

An earlier version of this chapter appeared in the February 2006 issue of *School Library Media Activities Monthly.*

Chapter 6
"Living Pictures": Tableau (Grades 4 and Up)

▪ INTRODUCTION

The previous chapter explored drama machines. A variation on the drama machine technique is tableau. *Tableau* is shorthand for *tableaux vivants* (tah-BLOW vee-VAHNT), a French phrase that translates to "living pictures." With tableau improvisations and activities, students create a frozen image to represent a moment in time, a historical photograph, or a painting.

In the United States, tableau first gained popularity as a Victorian-era parlor game in which partygoers would pose in elaborate costume as a living copy of a famous painting. Sometimes the posers would assemble behind a curtain, freeze in place, then be revealed when the curtain opened. This technique survives in some Christmas Nativity plays, in which participants pose as Old World masterpieces depicting the birth of Jesus. In Laguna Beach, California, the Pageant of the Masters uses elaborate sets, makeup, lighting, an annual budget of over $4 million, and a cast of over 300 to create tableaus that precisely re-create works of art (Navarro 2006).

Tableau is an established technique both for professional theatrical and operatic companies and as an educational tool (Kelner and Flynn 2006; Epstein 2004; Layne 2002; Wilhelm 2002). In the media center, tableaus can be performed in small student groups or be undertaken as a whole-class challenge. Tableaus can be relatively simple, as when replicating an Old World masterpiece, or more challenging, as when they are created by students in response to literature or research.

Though some tableau activities will incorporate movement, all begin as still images. This requires student focus and concentration, as well as the ability to sustain a physical position for some time. As a result, tableau has limited effectiveness with younger students and is best for students in grades 4 and up.

■ Simple Tableau: A Single Pose Based on a Photograph or Work of Art

Simple tableau takes an existing photograph or work of art and asks small groups of students to pose as the essential figures. Tableau also can be done with an entire class posing to replicate a work of art, but this requires higher levels of concentration. A simple tableau should take between 20 and 30 minutes, depending on the level of discussion between steps.

Simple tableau is a useful beginning exercise to introduce tableau to students. As an introduction, students may enjoy visiting the Pageant of the Masters Web site (http://www.foapom.com) to see elaborate examples and to become familiar with what is meant by the term *tableau.*

Step One: Collaborate to Select a Curriculum-Related Image

Collaborate with the classroom teacher or art specialist. Discuss his or her current curriculum units and find natural connections with tableau in the media center. Next, search for an image that represents a key idea or theme in that unit of study. (For this chapter, "image" is used as an umbrella term to describe any photograph, painting, watercolor, or book illustration.) A successful image for tableau will

- relate to the themes and key ideas of a curriculum unit;
- be clearly "readable" when projected via a data, opaque, or overhead projector; and
- contain several elements that can be portrayed by students.

When searching for images for potential tableaus, remember that students do not need to be limited to "human" roles. They can portray anything, including people, furniture, animals, or props. For example, in a painting of the Declaration of Independence, the document itself could be interpreted as the most important item, so it must be included.

▶ *Sources for Images*

Many current history and social studies books contain primary source images that can be used with a document projector for a simple tableau. Illustrations from literature anthologies, picture books, coffee table books, and nonfiction curriculum-related books are additional sources. The Internet has endless resources for images that can be used in simple tableau. The following Web sites are particularly recommended:

- American Memory, Library of Congress, http://memory.loc.gov: Enormous collection of primary source material from throughout American history. Particularly strong curriculum connections for the Gold Rush, Western Expansion, and the Civil War.
- AmericanRevolution.org, http://www.americanrevolution.org/artmain.html: Online gallery of artworks portraying the history of the American Revolution.

- Detroit Institute of Arts, www.dia.org: A strong survey collection of art, including Brueghel the Elder's *The Wedding Dance,* for a medieval history activity, a landscape collection for use with Western Expansion, and Diego Rivera's *Detroit Industry* frescoes for a lesson on industrialization or the twentieth century.

- The National Archives, http://www.archives.gov: Access to primary source documents. An education page at http://www.archives.gov/education organizes documents and images into historical periods compatible with school curricula.

- New York Public Library Digital, http://www.nypl.org/digital: Collection of nearly 500,000 digital images, including photos, manuscripts, and posters. Good for American history and culture.

- Pilgrim Hall Museum Online Gallery, http://www.pilgrimhall.org/hispaint.htm: Several paintings depicting various stages of the Pilgrims' journey to and arrival in the New World.

- Take One Picture Project, National Gallery, London, http://www.takeonepicture.org: Selected National Gallery artwork is chosen each year as the basis for classroom integration and exploration. The paintings have rich details that make them particularly interesting for tableau work. To see all paintings used in past projects, click on "The Picture." William Hogarth's 1724 painting *The Graham Children,* a scene of domesticity in an upper-class English family, is particularly well-suited for a large class because of the many allegorical elements present in the painting.

- Timeline of Art History, Metropolitan Museum of Art, http://www.metmuseum.org/toah/splash.htm: Western European artwork from across the centuries organized by time period. Strong collection of ancient Egyptian and Mesopotamian objects.

Step Two: Warm up the Students

Reawaken drama skills with a Welcoming Ritual and warm-up activities. "Make Me a . . ." and pantomime (see chapter 2) are particularly good warm-ups because they rely primarily on the body to express an idea.

Step Three: Display and Study the Image

Using a data projector, slide projector, poster-sized reproduction, or transparency, display the image in front of the class. Give the students a minute to examine the image in detail. Say,

This image was chosen because it has important lessons to teach us about (insert topic of study here). Sometimes, we can learn just as much from images as we can from words in books on the Internet. Take a moment to look at the image and see what you can learn about it.

Tip: If students have a difficult time focusing on the image, pass out scrap paper. Divide the class into small groups and set a timer or stopwatch for two minutes. Ask students to list all the items they can find in a picture: people, animals, furniture, flowers, and more. The National Archives' Education Department has excellent image analysis worksheets (http://www.archives.gov/education/lessons/) that can also help to focus the students' observation time. After two minutes are up, collect the scrap paper and congratulate the group with the most items on their list. This timed, competitive activity often motivates students to look more closely at the image than they otherwise would.

Step Four: Brainstorm the Most Important People and Objects in the Image

During a class's first exposure to tableau, the instructor plays an active role as "director" of the scene. Ask the class, "What are the most important objects or people in this image?" Write down a long list on the board. Then work with the students to narrow those choices to the top four or five items. This activity, in which students begin with a wide field of information and work to narrow it down to the most essential pieces, is useful practice for students who may have difficulty identifying the main idea of a reading passage or research quest. Remember to expand the list beyond human figures to include other objects in the image.

If the image already has a title, write the given title on the board. If not, ask students to brainstorm a title for the image. Write their ideas on the board. Then select the one you are going to use. Also, write the name of the artist or photographer on the board.

Step Five: With the Instructor Acting as the Director, Position Students in the Tableau

Look back at the projected image. Pose the most important object first. Say, "If you would like to be the _____, please put your hand up now." As discussed in chapter 3, casting as the tableau progresses is more time efficient, and it holds student attention and enthusiasm more effectively.

Continue positioning each character in a rough placement. Refine positions when everyone is in place. Be sure to discuss where each student's eyes should be focusing. Sometimes this is easy to discover: If two figures in the image are looking at each other, the two student actors should do the same. When students are portraying nonhuman objects, this becomes more subjective. For example, should the child playing the table in a Vermeer painting be looking at the human figures or away? Up or down? This can be decided collaboratively between students and instructors. Talking should be kept to a minimum.

Tip: When posing the figures, the natural instinct is to ask them to pose in front of the projected image, as if stepping into the shoes of the character. While this does make the instructor/director's job easier, it is uncomfortable for the student performers to have bright lights shining in their eyes. Instead, pose students to one side of the image, or ask them to stand opposite the image so that *they* can see the image. In this case, the tableau they make will be a mirror image of the original, while allowing the student performers to compare their own work to that of the original and to "edit" their own presentation.

Step Six: Use Varying Levels to Refine the Tableau

Many young performers tend to "just stand" when first placed in a tableau, which makes it lackluster and rarely mimics the original image. Point out opportunities for particular performers to pose at varying levels—low, medium, or high—to improve the visual composition of the picture and promote interest.

Step Seven: Present Initial Performance

Create an audio signal to begin and end the tableau. A beat of a drum, the playing of a triangle, the tinkling of a bell, or a hand clap are all possible signals. Demonstrate the signal to the students and explain that you will begin the tableau by giving the signal once. When the performers hear the signal, they will speak the title of the image in strong, assertive voices. They will then hold the pose silently for a few seconds until the instructor gives the signal again. After the second signal, they should call out the name of the artist or photographer. This concludes the simple tableau. The concept of titling the tableau and signaling to begin or end it comes from teaching artist Sean Layne and his Kennedy Center instructional video (2001–2002) that focuses specifically on tableaus for classroom use and workshops for teachers and students. Kelner and Flynn (2006) use the word "action" to begin the tableau and the word "freeze" to end it.

Step Eight: Debrief, Receive Feedback, and Revise

Next, invite the performers to relax their bodies while leading a debriefing discussion using the "sandwiching" technique discussed in chapter 5. This layering of constructive criticism between positive comments is effective because it tells the performers not only where improvements could be made, but also what elements of the tableau are effective and should be kept. Give the performers no more than two minutes to confer and revise.

Step Nine: Present Revised Performance

Repeat the performance using the process listed in Step Seven.

Step Ten: Think and Reflect

Now that students have experienced the tableau physically and kinesthetically (if they were in the tableau) or visually (if they observed it), they are ready to draw some inferences and discuss the *content* of the tableau. The following questions can help to engage students and connect the drama activity to the curriculum:

- What do you think the artist wanted us to know about this picture?
- What do you think her purpose was? To tell a story? To convince us? To record a piece of history?
- Why do you think this character was facing in that direction? What are we supposed to learn about that person from that position?
- Why was so-and-so positioned in the back/front/middle/edge of the tableau?
- Who is the main subject of the painting? How can you tell?
- What can we learn about American history/this famous person/this work of literature from this tableau?

Because this activity does not involve every student, it is better classified as an exploratory project, not as an assessed activity. However, all students—both those who are observing and those who are in the tableau—will benefit from the opportunity to evaluate and reflect on what has been learned. This metacognition is an important component of an arts-integrated lesson plan (Kelner and Flynn 2006) and of reading comprehension (McMaster 1998). This reflection is also consistent with information literacy models that call upon students to reflect on the success of their process and product.

The student reflection worksheet (page 105) provides a quick opportunity for student metacognition and reflection.

Whole Class Extensions

Once a simple tableau has been modeled by a small group, it can be expanded into a whole class activity in two different ways. First is to divide an image into several smaller images. To do so, print out an image and cut it into smaller detail sections, giving each section to a group from the class. Brueghel's paintings, referenced above, are an excellent example of a larger work from which five or six smaller details could be taken. Divide the class into groups of three to five students each. In each group, assign one student to be the director (the role played by the media specialist in the previous example) and the others to create the tableau. The students examine their given segment, decide on the important elements, decide on a subtitle for their segment, and pose themselves under the leadership of their student director. After rehearsal time, the media specialist brings the class together and positions the groups to create the whole original image. The media specialist uses the preestablished signal to begin the tableau, and the entire class calls out the name of the painting. Then, using a technique Wilhelm (2002) calls "tapping in" and Kelner and Flynn (2006) call "shoulder touch," the media specialist moves among the groups. When the media specialist taps the shoulder of a group member, the entire group calls out the subtitle in unison. When all groups have called out their titles, the media specialist signals again, and the simple tableau ends with the name of the artist. Further rehearsals can focus on

- groups adding interesting *vocal variety* by varying the pitch, speed, volume, or tone of their title;
- making a clear choice about *eye focus,* or where each participant is looking or focusing;
- adjusting body positioning to incorporate low, medium, and high *levels*; and
- brainstorming an appropriate *sequence* for each smaller tableau.

This technique is useful because students are put in charge of their own inquiry and exploration process and because dividing the class into small groups keeps all students active. Allow 45 minutes for this technique and be sure to allow time for debriefing and reflection (see the reflection worksheet on page 105).

Reflection: Tableau

Name: _____

1. How would you **describe the technique of Tableau** to someone who had never seen it before?

2. What did you **learn about our unit of study** from today's activity?

3. What **new questions** do you have?

4. What is one **strategy** to make Tableau more interesting to the audience?

■ SPEED TABLEAU: EXPLORING THEMES

This technique comes from Virginia Grainger, a theatre educator with the Royal Shakespeare Company, and is recommended for students in grades 4 and up. She uses this activity to quickly acquaint students with the major themes of a play prior to studying the play with them in depth.

Speed tableaus are created in rapid-fire succession. Students must work quickly to build consensus and create their pose. This can often "force" timid students into making a decision and acting on it. Students work in small groups, and each group responds simultaneously to the instructions, keeping all students engaged for the entirety of the activity. This activity can be done in as little as 20 minutes and is an excellent introduction to an instructional unit or research project, as it can quickly introduce students to a series of themes or key ideas. Because the themes and ideas are stored in students' muscle memory, not just in their cerebral memory, they can be recalled with far greater ease as the unit of study continues. Because the thematic connections are announced in advance, students are more alert and more likely to connect disparate items thematically.

Step One: Create a List of Five Themes or Key Concepts from a Curriculum Unit

Work collaboratively to identify the area to be explored. Choose a topic broad enough to have at least five distinct themes or ideas from the unit of study that students should understand by the conclusion of the unit. Although the unit of study may be new to students, the five ideas should be familiar to them. For example, if the unit of study is Western Expansion, students may not have prior knowledge about the terms "Louisiana Purchase" or "Lewis and Clark," but they would likely be familiar with a more general term like "exploration." Themes or concepts can range from concrete ideas (example: train) to abstract concepts (example: fear). Sequence the five items from the most concrete to the most abstract. Success with the earlier concrete tasks will bolster students' confidence for the later, more abstract ones.

▶ *Sample Speed Tableau Topics—Literature*

The Miraculous Journey of Edward Tulane, by Kate Di Camillo: love, loss, loneliness, hate, relief

Show Way, Jacqueline Woodson, illustrated by Hudson Talbott: slavery, civil rights, Underground Railroad, ancestors, daughter

Island of the Blue Dolphins, by Scott O'Dell: being alone, caring for yourself, companionship, sadness, rescue

The Diary of Anne Frank: silence, writing, family, secrets, danger

▶ *Sample Speed Tableau Topics—History*

Harriet Tubman/slavery: master, slave, separation from family, freedom, escape

Western Expansion: growing, exploration, new place, leaving home, looking for riches

Civil War: brother against brother, slavery, many dead, Abraham Lincoln, state history: top exports, landmarks, land forms, or famous citizens

Three branches of government (this one gets only three themes!): executive, legislative, judicial

Step Two: Lead Students in Warm-up Activities

Five minutes' worth of activities is adequate for this project. Focus on *body* activities.

Step Three: Divide the Class into Groups of Three to Five Students

Distribute the groups throughout the playing space. Experiment with assigning students randomly into groups instead of letting them select their own group members. By switching around groups, students encounter new methods of working and can generate new, creative ideas.

Step Four: Give Instructions

Say,

We are going to play a tableau game called speed tableau. As you know from our past tableau work, a tableau is a frozen picture that communicates information. I am going to call out five words. After each word, I will give you one minute to work with your group to create a tableau of that word. Make a decision quickly and get working on making the tableau shape. Remember to think about low, medium, and high levels that can make your tableau much more expressive and interesting. This is a body language exercise, not a voice exercise—your goal is to create a silent, frozen statue about the word I call out.

Step Five: Establish the Five Tableaus

Call out each word and give students one minute to create that tableau. For speed tableau, do not pause between each theme to give students a chance to observe one another. That opportunity will come later in the activity.

Step Six: Speed Tableau

Say,

> Now I'll repeat the themes in random order. Move as quickly as you can from one to the next.

Call out the themes quickly and randomly, changing themes every five to ten seconds, until each theme has been called at least three times and each group has memorized the tableau poses. These fast repetitions give the groups plenty of practice in forming and refining their tableaus.

Step Seven: Group Sequencing

Say,

> Now I'm going to give you five minutes to put the five themes in an order that makes sense to you. You should pose in each position for five seconds. Then move to the next tableau. Find an interesting way to move your bodies so that you make an interesting transition—or movement pattern—between each tableau. You may discuss your ideas with your group members using quiet voices.

During the five minutes of work time, instructors move throughout the groups providing guidance and support, watching for interesting levels or groups who are struggling to communicate and need instructor intervention.

Step Eight: Share Presentations

Each group comes before the class and presents its tableau sequences silently. Ask each group to let the class know when they are ready to begin and remind the students of expected audience behavior (see earlier chapters). At the conclusion of each presentation, ask members of the class to guess each of the five themes and provide feedback. Because this is a rapid exercise, and students have multiple opportunities to refine their tableaus during the preparation period, there is no second presentation.

Step Nine: Reflection and Evaluation

This activity is most effective as a content exploration activity followed by instructor-led discussion introducing the new curriculum unit. If student self-reflection is desired, distribute the tableau reflection sheet (page 105).

■ TEXT TABLEAU: DEEPENING COMPREHENSION OF TEXT

In addition to exploring visual content and themes, tableau is also useful to help students break down larger, complicated texts into smaller chunks for higher levels of comprehension.

A traditional approach to a complicated text might be for the instructor to consume an entire class period doing a detailed, nearly line-by-line textual reading. But in the text tableau method, the text is excerpted into small chunks, one for each student group. Each group is responsible for creating a tableau that represents that portion of the text.

This approach differs from simple tableau because it places the responsibility for making compositional and comprehension choices in the hands of students. Rather than acting as "director," the media specialist is transformed into a guide who outlines the steps, keeps track of time, and provides feedback, but allows the students to create their own tableau.

After rehearsals are completed, the groups are reunited in a half-circle shape in sequential order. The small group tableaus are performed in order. The physicalization of the text makes it more accessible to the rest of the class, and the intensive work done by each group strengthens their comprehension. Allow 40 minutes to one hour for this activity.

To illuminate this technique, the Preamble to the United States Constitution is used as the source text (page 110). Text tableau provides a fun way for elementary students to engage with this difficult text.

Text Tableau: Preamble to the U.S. Constitution

Name: _____

We, the people of the United States,

in order to form a more perfect Union,

establish justice,

insure domestic tranquility,

provide for the common defense,

promote the general welfare, and

secure the blessings of liberty to ourselves and our posterity,

do ordain and establish this Constitution for the United States of America.

Step One: Collaborate to Select a Curriculum-Related Text

When selecting text for use with an upper elementary class, look for text that has approximately one key idea for each group of students. Once this technique has been tried with a class, it can be expanded so that each group has two or three ideas to tableau and put into a sequence, but for the first attempt, start with a single idea per group.

Lay out the text so that it can be scanned easily by the students. For example, the Preamble to the U.S. Constitution is written in paragraph or prose form. In the worksheet (page 110), the Preamble is reformatted on the page so that there is only one key idea per line. This helps young learners break complex sentences into smaller, more manageable pieces.

To follow this lesson plan, photocopy the performance reflection sheet on page 114 onto the reverse of the Constitution worksheet (page 110).

Step Two: Warm up the Group

Select warm-up exercises from chapter 2 that build body flexibility and agility.

Step Three: Split the Text into Parts and Assign Groups

The text of the Preamble (page 110) is distributed to each student (along with a highlighter or colored pencil) as well as being made into a transparency.

The media specialist works with the class to decipher the main ideas of the Constitution. Key words are identified by the class and underlined by the media specialist on the transparency.

The classroom teacher reads the text aloud once to the class, including the text's title, pausing to discuss unfamiliar vocabulary. In the case of the Constitution, words like "union" and "tranquility" may be outside the working vocabulary of many students.

Now the media specialist and classroom teacher work with the students to assign groups of three to five students each, and a phrase to each group. In this case, the class decides that the opening words, "We, the people, of the United States" and the closing words "do ordain and establish this Constitution for the United States of America" will be spoken chorally, in unison, by the entire class instead of announcing the title. The rest of the lines will be assigned to different groups. This is noted on the worksheet, and students use their highlighters or colored pencils to denote their assigned text.

At the conclusion of this activity, the overhead transparency has been annotated and looks like this:

Text Tableau:
Preamble to the
U.S. Constitution

Name:
Overhead Transparency

We, the people of the United States, *Everyone - start when hear bell*

in order to form a more perfect Union, *Group 1: Tony, Julie, Quinton, Don*

establish justice, *Group 2: Rob, Maja, Kerry, Bernadette*

insure domestic tranquility, *Group 3: Abby, Bob, Chris, Mindy, Louis*

provide for the common defense, *Group 4: Annie, Quincy, Elise, Karina*

promote the general welfare, and *Group 5: George, Ailie, Lucy, Jack*

Group 6: Grace, Mark E, Karl, Adam

secure the blessings of liberty to ourselves and our posterity,

do ordain and establish this Constitution for the United States of America.

Everyone - speak when hear bell

Step Four: Review the Elements of Text Tableau

Now the media specialist and classroom teacher assign ground rules for the text tableau. The instructor says,

---

This activity is called text tableau. We have done tableau projects before. Text tableau is like some tableau projects because it begins with a frozen pose, like a statue, and it ends with a frozen pose.

Remember that low, medium, and high levels will make a more interesting composition, or picture.

What makes text tableau different is that you can come to life in the middle of your tableau, while you are speaking the assigned words. To make sure that the meaning is understood, each group must come up with a way of saying their text. It might be said just by one participant, spoken at the same time by the whole group (this is considered "choral work"), or students may take turns with various words. Remember that varying the pitch, volume, speed, and tone of your voices helps to communicate the words. The words we underlined together were the words we agreed were the most important, so give them extra emphasis.

You have five minutes to plan your tableau. When the planning time is up, we'll gather in a half-circle and watch the tableaus in order.

Step Five: Give Students Five Minutes to Work Together to Build the Tableau

While the groups work, the instructors circle among them, assisting "stuck" groups, reminding students about levels, and making sure that the work being done is representative of the assigned text. (Unfocused or uncomfortable students may feel the urge to aim for goofy outbursts instead of sustained, focused presentations. Guidance from the instructors can curtail this.)

Step Six: Initial Presentation

After the planning time is up, the instructors arrange the groups in sequential order in a half-circle. This shape allows each group to see all of the other groups, and, if this improvisational activity transforms into a formal performance, the half-circle will also enable the audience to see every group.

The instructor says,

We will begin the text tableau when I ring the bell. When you hear the bell, say the opening words that we agreed on together: "We, the people of the United States." Let's try that. *(Rehearse this.)*

Then we will start at the far left end of the semicircle and watch each group come to life as it presents its piece of text. When the last group has finished, listen for the bell again. Then we will say the last words together: "do ordain and establish this Constitution of the United States." That will end our text tableau.

Step Seven: Student Self-Evaluation

There are many possibilities for feedback and reflection here. For this exercise, the four-panel performance feedback sheet (page 114) is useful. This activity again builds on student metacognition. As students become more skilled at self-evaluation, they are better able to see a performance and know what to do to improve it without teacher intervention. The performance feedback sheet empowers students to reflect privately on their practice and the practice of those in their group. Note how the four sections of the reflection sheet keep the tone positive by avoiding such questions as, "What did you mess up?" or "Who messed up?"

Students who fill in at least one idea for each of the four sections, as shown on page 115, will be prepared to enter the revision stage with concrete ideas for improvement.

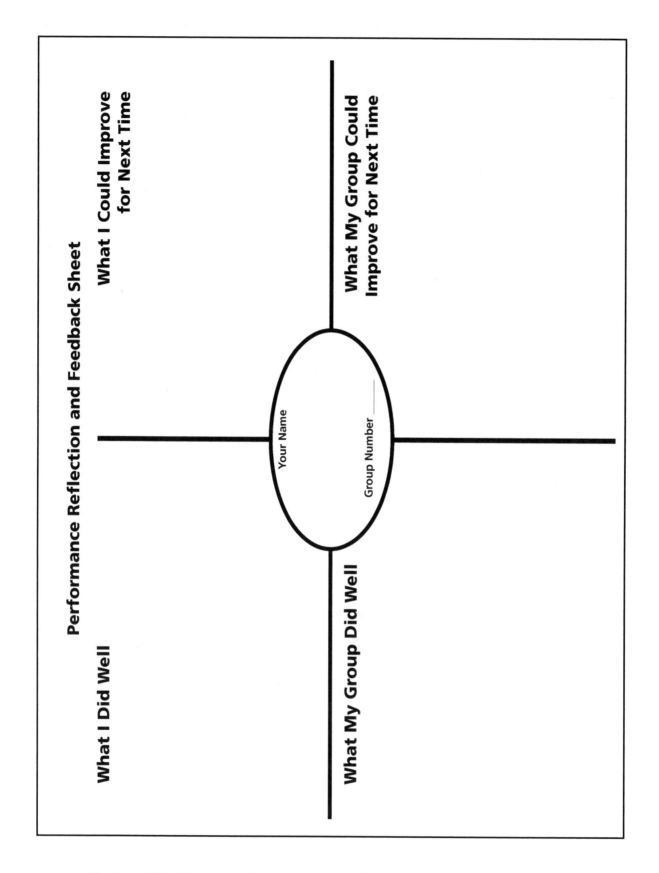

Performance Reflection and Feedback Sheet

What I Could Improve for Next Time

What My Group Could Improve for Next Time

Your Name

Group Number _____

What I Did Well

What My Group Did Well

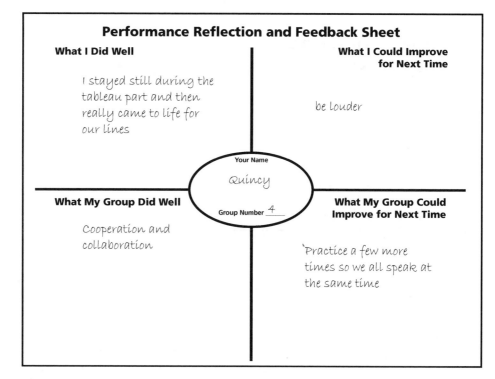

Step Eight: Revised Performance

Repeat the performance using the process listed in Step Six.

Step Nine: Evaluation.

To evaluate a text tableau, consider the text tableau assessment rubric (page 116), which can be completed first by the student and then by the instructors. Assessment for this activity takes three areas into consideration: acting skills (body, voice, and imagination); teamwork skills (concentration and cooperation); and content understanding.

Assessment Rubric: Text Tableau

Name _____

Class _____

For each category, give yourself a score of between 1 (very low) and 10 (outstanding).

Place your score in the Self-Evaluation column.

Your teachers will also score you in the Teacher Evaluation column.

How well did you . . .	Self-Evaluation	Teacher Evaluation
Use vocal variety such as pitch, volume, and speed to make your text delivery interesting and easy to understand?		
Create a tableau pose that was specific and clear?		
Focus your eyes on a specific point?		
Contribute to class discussions?		
Work cooperatively with your group to plan and create the tableau?		
Contribute your fair share to the group's work?		
Work quietly and productively, without distracting others from their work?		
Use your time wisely so you were ready to perform when asked?		
Create a tableau that showed that you understood the meaning of your text?		
Use the reflection process to improve your final tableau?		
Final Score (out of 100):		

Other Texts Suitable for Text Tableau

> • **Dr. Martin Luther King Jr.'s "I have a dream" speech.** Choose an excerpt rather than attempting the entire speech.
>
> • **Historical documents.** After studying a larger primary document such as the Declaration of Independence, constitutional amendments, slavery documents, feudal arrangements during medieval times, or pioneer homesteading laws, work with students to list the most salient points for text tableau.
>
> • **School mission statement.** Many schools post their building or district mission statement in the lobby, but using a text tableau to bring it to life can help students absorb its meaning. Consider sharing this at an assembly or PTA meeting.
>
> • **School behavioral expectations.** Similarly, a text tableau can help students understand school rules. Ask older students to prepare a text tableau to share with younger students.

MORPHING TABLEAU

"Morphing" is a computer graphics and animation term that refers to one image that slowly distorts and changes until it becomes a second image. Morphing tableau is also referred to as "Slideshow Tableau" (Wilhelm 2002) or "Human Slide Show" (Kelner and Flynn 2006).

Morphing tableau is a student-created form of tableau. Small groups of three to five students work together to create four or five static tableau positions and a "headline" that introduces each one.

Like text tableau, levels, vocal energy, and having a clear focus clarify and improve the procedure, but each morphing tableau project stands alone. It is not woven into an overall class project.

When the series of tableaus has been sequenced and mastered, the group then works to find a way to transition smoothly from one tableau to the next—in other words, morphing! Each "morph" should be fluid, without startling moves, a drastic energy contrast with the unmoving, frozen tableau. One explanation that can help students envision this activity is to compare it to a PowerPoint™ slide show. In PowerPoint, interesting transitions can be programmed between slides. In a morphing tableau, the transitions should be as well-planned as the individual tableaus themselves.

Students can create morphing tableaus to show a sequence of events in a story, steps in a scientific process, the progression of battles, or a series of causes that led to a particular effect. The topic for each tableau can be instructor-directed or, for more of a challenge, the student groups can identify the key moments and create morphing tableaus around them. Morphing tableau can be a useful end-of-unit activity because it calls on students to recall, restate, retell, summarize, sequence, and synthesize key events.

Students can use the tableau planning sheet (page 118) to quickly organize and sequence their thoughts and ideas. Allow visual learners to sketch the tableaus in lieu of writing out their descriptions.

Planning Sheet:
Morphing Tableau

Subject of tableau _____

Use words or drawings to plan each of your five tableaus.
When you rehearse, remember to add an interesting "morph"
or transition between each tableau!

Group Members:

_____
_____
_____
_____

1

2

3

4

5

Follow the steps outlined for the prior tableau techniques, allowing time for student reflection between the first and second presentations. One change comes in the final presentation, in which tableau participants are randomly selected to respond to the tableau. This addition is called awakening the tableau.

Awakening the Tableau: Adding Voice to Participants in a Tableau

Awakening is a technique that can be added to morphing or simple tableau activities. When a tableau observer enters the tableau and taps a participant in the tableau, the participant "comes alive" and shares text. This action is used by many tableau practitioners, including Layne (2002); Wilhelm (2002), who refers to it as "tapping in"; and Kelner and Flynn (2006), who call it "shoulder touch." I prefer the term "awakening," because it helps students visualize the transition from a frozen to an animated state.

The "awakener" can be the media specialist, a classroom teacher, or a selected student. Groups presenting tableaus are alerted in advance to hold each pose for five seconds before morphing to the next tableau. During this time, the awakener may enter the tableau and gently touch a participant on the shoulder or arm. When the participant is touched, he or she "awakens," relaxing his or her body out of the pose. The participant then prepares to answer a question *in character* from the awakener.

Imagine that a group is presenting a morphing tableau showing moments from the chapter book *Charlotte's Web,* by E. B. White. One of the tableaus features the beginning of chapter 11, when Lurvy has just brought Mr. Zuckerman to the barn to see Charlotte's first word web. One student is playing the dumbstruck Lurvy; one is the amazed Mr. Zuckerman; one is looking on at the drowsy Charlotte, tired from her overnight weavings; one is Wilbur, standing right under the web; and one student, Jennie, has contorted her arms, legs, and fingers into angular shapes to portray the web.

A teacher or student awakener taps Jennie. The awakener might ask Jennie (in character as the spider web) to

- **Introduce herself.** Sample response: "I'm the spider web." (If the student were to answer, "Jennie," the instructor might step in to clarify that all answers should be given in the character and voice of the spider web.)

- **Explain her character's importance to the overall work of literature.** Sample response: "Charlotte wove me to draw attention to Wilbur and to save his life." (A less developed answer such as, "Because spiders weave webs," which is factually true but does not relate to *Charlotte's Web,* would require a follow-up question from the instructor.)

- **Explain what is happening at the moment the scene was frozen into tableau.** Sample response: "Charlotte wove this web to get some attention for Wilbur, so he won't get killed."

- **Explain what might happen next.** Example: "Charlotte's webs will make Wilbur famous."

Tip: Post these categories on large pieces of chart paper so that they can be seen by the awakeners.

After a successful answer is given, the awakener moves on to another participant in the tableau. Because it may be difficult for young performers to hold a pose for very long, limit each tableau to a single question and appoint only one awakener for each group. Avoid swapping out student awakeners during a single morphing tableau, as it forces participants to pose for too long.

These spontaneous questions call on higher-level thinking skills. Not only must participants be prepared to identify their characters and the events of the scene, but they must place both character and the scene in the greater context of the novel. Finally, they must understand how this chapter's events affect future events in the novel, understanding how events are interrelated.

Variation for Younger Students

Honolulu's Pacific Resources for Education and Learning organization uses drama for English as a Second Language learners. Its Web-based videos (http://www.prel.org/eslstrategies/drama.html) demonstrate a variation on morphing tableaus. Rather than asking students to create slow, sustained transitions between tableaus, the instructor quickly taps together two drumsticks as the children hurry to place themselves in the next tableau.

Evaluation

To evaluate a morphing tableau, use the morphing tableau assessment rubric (page 121) for student and teacher evaluation.

Assessment Rubric: Morphing Tableaus

Name _____

Class _____

For each category, give yourself a score of between 1 (very low) and 10 (outstanding).

Place your score in the Self-Evaluation column.

Your teachers will also score you in the Teacher Evaluation column.

How well did you . . .	Self-Evaluation	Teacher Evaluation
Use vocal variety such as pitch, volume, and speed to make your text delivery interesting and easy to understand?		
Create tableau poses that were specific, clear, and frozen, with clear eye focus?		
"Morph" effectively from one pose to the next, using fluid movements?		
Select meaningful scenes for tableau?		
Answer questions posed by the awakener?		
Work cooperatively with your group and the class to plan and create the tableaus, contributing your fair share?		
Work quietly and productively, without distracting others from their work?		
Use your time wisely so you were ready to perform when asked?		
Create a tableau that showed that you understood the meaning of each scene?		
Use the reflection process to improve your final tableau?		
Final Score (out of 100):		

■ ONLINE RESOURCES FOR TABLEAU

Tableau is best understood when it is seen. Several online examples will help your students envision and understand the tableau concept.

Making Meaning in Literature (2003) is an online video course by Annenberg Media's Learner.org site that shows a variety of comprehension strategies in middle grade language arts classes. Episode Six of the series focuses on the classroom of Dr. Jan Currence and demonstrates how she uses tableau and awakening to bring Christopher Paul Curtis's *The Watsons Go to Birmingham—1963* to life. The series is available at http://www.learner.org/resources/series169.html. A free registration is required.

Schools with a paid subscription to the UnitedStreaming digital video service (http://www.unitedstreaming.com) can enter "Tableau" in the search box to find the video *Teacher to Teacher: Professional Development for Today's Classroom: Language Arts, Volume II.* This series' third segment, *Integrating Drama into Language Arts & Social Studies,* shows how Melanie Rick, a fourth-grade teacher in suburban Washington, D.C., uses Sean Layne's "Actor's Ritual" and tableau techniques to help her students better comprehend Virginia history.

Layne's techniques are also available by purchasing *Living Pictures: A Theatrical Technique for Learning Across the Curriculum,* a VHS video from the Kennedy Center. Visit http://www.kennedy-center.org/education/pdot/livingpictures/video_workshop.html to order.

The Pacific Resources for Learning organization's Web page *Telling Stories: Using Drama and Multimedia with ESL Students* (http://www.prel.org/esltrategies/drama.html) has several brief QuickTime clips showing tableau strategies.

■ CONCLUSION

Tableau is an effective comprehension skill because it requires students to sift through content and select key moments and relevant information. Students connect moments, find meaning in textual or visual elements, and sequence events.

Working together, they meet deadlines, creating original, motivating products that avoid plagiarism. They use their growing acting skills to create visually appealing compositions with interesting vocal components.

■ REFERENCES

Annenberg Media/Maryland Public Television. 2003. "Part 6: Dramatic Tableaux." In *Making Meaning in Literature.* Available at http://www.learner.org/resources/series169.html (accessed August 28, 2006).

Di Camillo, Kate. 2006. *The Mysterious Journey of Edward Tulane.* Cambridge, MA: Candlewick. 198pp. ISBN 0763625892.

Discovery Channel School. 2005. *Teacher to Teacher: Professional Development for Today's Classroom: Language Arts Volume II.* Available at http://www. unitedstreaming.com/ (accessed August 28, 2006).

Epstein, Shira D. 2004. "Reimagining Literary Practices: Creating Living Midrash from Ancient Texts Through Tableau." *Journal of Jewish Education* 70(1/2) (Summer).

Festival of Arts Web site. http://foapom.com (accessed August 28, 2006).

Frank, Anne. 1995. *The Diary of a Young Girl: The Definitive Edition.* New York: Doubleday. 340pp. ISBN 0385473788; 038542695X.

Kelner, Lenore Blank, and, Flynn, Rosalind. 2006. *A Dramatic Approach to Reading Comprehension.* Portsmouth, NH: Heinemann. 229pp. ISBN 0325007942.

Kennedy Center. 2007. *Teaching Tableau.* Available at http://artsedge.kennedy-center. org/content/3933/index.html (accessed January 16, 2007)

King, Martin Luther, Jr. 1997. *I Have a Dream.* Illustrated by Kathleen A. Wilson. New York: Scholastic. 20pp. ISBN 0590205161.

Layne, Sean. 2001–2002. *Living Pictures: A Theatrical Technique for Learning Across the Curriculum* (videorecording). Washington, DC: Kennedy Center.

McMaster, Jennifer Catney. 1998. "'Doing' Literature: Using Drama to Build Literacy." *The Reading Teacher* 51(7): 574–580.

National Archives Education Department. n.d. *Teaching with Documents: Lesson Plans.* Available at http://www.archives.gov/education/lessons/ (accessed August 28, 2006).

Navarro, Mireya. 2006. "The Tableau Vivant Is Alive and Well and Living in Laguna Beach." *New York Times* (online), August 1.

O'Dell, Scott. 1990 (c1960). *Island of the Blue Dolphins.* Boston: Houghton Mifflin. 181pp. ISBN 039553680.

Pacific Resources for Learning. 2005. *Telling Stories: Using Drama and Multimedia with ESL Students.* Available at http://www.prel.org/eslstrategies/drama.html (accessed August 14, 2006)

Wilhelm, Jeffrey D. 2002. *Action Strategies for Deepening Comprehension.* New York: Scholastic Professional. 192pp. ISBN 0439218578.

Woodson, Jacqueline. 2005. *Show Way.* Illustrated by Hudson Talbott. New York: G. P. Putnam. unpaged. ISBN 0399239496.

Chapter 7
Putting It Together: Living Newspapers (Grades 5 and Up)

■ INTRODUCTION

Long before FTP stood for the Internet's File Transfer Protocol, it stood for the Federal Theatre Project. During the Great Depression, many federal projects were established to create jobs for the otherwise unemployed. One of these was the Federal Theatre Project, led by Vassar theatre professor Hallie Flanagan. As the better-known Works Progress Administration or the Civilian Conservation Corps were for other types of workers, the Federal Theatre Project was established with the purpose of keeping America's artists, actors, and theatrical employees working during the Depression.

The FTP was amazingly wide-reaching in its range of supported projects: marionettes to Shakespeare, opera to children's theatre, African American troupes to Yiddish theatre, even *The Hot Mikado,* a jazz remake of the classic Gilbert and Sullivan operetta. Some of its best-known participants were actors Orson Welles and John Houseman and playwrights Clifford Odets and Archibald MacLeish.

One of the missions of the Federal Theatre Project was to use theatre as a means of sharing information. (In retrospect, this was perhaps its downfall, as some in Washington felt the FTP was overly political in the works it promoted. Cinema buffs might recall the recent film *The Cradle Will Rock,* a historical film examining the political scuffle surrounding the government's withdrawal of support for an FTP play of the same name.)

Among its information-sharing projects was the establishment of "Living Newspaper" projects. The goal of the Living Newspaper was to collect a series of stories surrounding a single theme and, instead of publishing them in print, to dramatize them and share them. Living Newspapers shared many of the same elements as their print counterparts: statistics, comics, economics, editorials, and historical background. Hallie Flanagan argued that Living Newspapers could adopt a point of view and should leave their audiences pondering questions about the theme. However, she was adamant that Living Newspapers should be rooted in fact, something she emphasized when testifying before the House Un-American Activities Committee in 1938 (Bentley 1988).

The Living Newspapers' most famous project was called *Power!* and traced the history of electric power from its discovery through the then-recent Tennessee Valley Authority project to transform rural regions of America by bringing electrical power to them.

Writers of Living Newspapers researched ideas thoroughly before creating a series of sketches, skits, pantomimes, and projections (Bentley 1988; Flanagan 1940). Scripts were fact-checked prior to rehearsal (Bentley 1988).

The Living Newspaper was effective then, and the same drama technique is effective today. Like the wax museum, described in chapter 4, the living newspaper is primarily a performance project. While improvisation is part of the planning process, the living newspaper is meant to be a more polished and performed work. Like a real newspaper, which collects several stories in a single edition, a living newspaper collects several dramatic skits and connects them with an overall theme.

■ WHAT DOES A LIVING NEWSPAPER CLASS PROJECT LOOK LIKE?

With student-created living newspapers, a central theme is selected. For school purposes, this would be rooted in a curriculum theme. Once the theme is selected, the class is divided into several research groups. Each research group develops a particular area of interest and creates a brief skit or monologue based on one of the techniques explored earlier in this book: wax museum, narrative pantomime, or tableau. As in the tableau technique (chapter 6), each group creates a headline that is performed by the group to begin and end their scene. The instructional team guides the process but stops short of directing it. Choices about how to portray each scene are made principally by the students. Because of the level of independence required, this activity is recommended for grades 5 and up.

■ CREATING A LIVING NEWSPAPER

Step One: Consult with a Collaborating Teacher and Select a Topic

When considering the overarching topic, be sure to select one that can be subdivided into several subtopics, each with a unique and different perspective. The theme can be a literal time frame—such as a decade—or a thematic one, such as Western Expansion. Here are some possible themes and subcategories for a living newspaper:

- **Western Expansion:** Gold Rush, Levi Strauss, Transcontinental Railroad, Oregon Trail, Lewis and Clark
- **Civil rights:** The "I have a dream" speech, Memphis sanitation workers' strike, Selma march, "Letters from a Birmingham Jail," Montgomery bus boycott, Birmingham church bombing, Malcolm X, Black Panthers, assassination of Martin Luther King Jr.
- **Turn of the century:** Gibson girls, Henry Ford and the assembly line, Wright brothers/first flight, Jack Johnson and the color barrier, women's suffrage

> • Pioneers: covered wagons, Mormon Trail, life on the trail, food on the trail, supplies needed

Type up the list of potential topics for students to choose from. Have more topics on the list than there will be groups in the class so no group feels it got the "leftover" topic. Students may also propose an alternate topic for the instructors to approve.

Step Two: Develop the Rubric and Project Timeline

As explained previously, planning the rubric up front has many advantages. A rubric for the living newspaper should reflect the stages of the project: research, writing/preparation, rehearsals, and performance. For it to be an arts-integrated project, it should be evaluated both as an artistic piece and as an academic project.

The tableau chapter discusses how self-evaluation in drama can help students' metacognition skills, their ability to think about their own work and work processes. The sample assessment rubric for a living newspaper builds on this concept by allowing students to self-select two goals that will be evaluated. When students are asked to identify two goals for themselves, they must reflect on their current skill levels and visualize themselves as having more success in those areas. McMaster (1998) notes the importance of visualization for reading comprehension. Involving students in both the creation and execution of a rubric can increase their motivation and their commitment to a project.

As noted on the rubric (page 128), students can select goals from the following categories: acting goals, research goals, and writing goals. Many students are not used to being asked to identify skills for self-evaluation. The following list of skills may help jumpstart students' thinking:

Sample Acting Goals	Sample Research Goals	Sample Writing Goals
• To speak loudly and clearly. • To use levels in my body. • To show emotion in my face. • To look at the actor who is talking to me. • To have good posture. • To try a character voice that is very different from my own. • To slow down when speaking. • To memorize my entire script before the first whole-class rehearsal.	• To highlight the main idea of a reading passage on my printouts. • To identify two good surface web resources. • To navigate a subscription encyclopedia and add information from it to my research. • To use a subscription database independently to find at least two articles.	• To outline our script using correct scriptwriting conventions. • To write with proper capitalization (and/or spelling and/or grammar). • To type my script without errors. • To structure my scene so it has (choose one or more): exposition, rising action, climax, falling action, and a conclusion.

Assessment Rubric: Living Newspaper

Name _____

Class _____

Before Beginning the Living Newspaper Project:
Your instructors have assigned eight out of ten evaluation categories for this assignment. Before beginning this project, you will set two personal goals that you hope to achieve for this project. They can be acting goals, research goals, or writing goals. Write each goal in the blank space given on the chart below and ask an instructor to date and initial it.

During the Living Newspaper Project:
Check your work against the rubric to be sure that your project is progressing towards the goals you and your teacher have set for the project.

After the final Living Newspaper Performance:
Evaluate yourself in the "Self Evaluation" column by giving yourself a score of between 1 (very low) and 10 (outstanding). Turn in your Project Folder (containing all research and the Planning Sheet in the right pocket). This rubric should be the *only thing* in the left pocket.

How well did you . . .	Self Evaluation	Teacher Evaluation
Use vocal variety such as pitch, volume, and speed to make your text delivery interesting and easy to understand?		
Use body poses and body language that were specific and clear, with a specific eye focus?		
Use research to create a historically accurate scene that was well-written, with strong details?		
Work quietly and productively, without distracting others from their work, keeping track of your work with your Planning Sheet and Project Folder?		
Keep track of your project, using and turning in your research, Planning Sheet, and Project Folder?		
Work cooperatively to plan and create the scene, headline, and overall Living Newspaper? Did you contribute your fair share to the group and the class?		
Use your time wisely so you were ready to perform when asked?		
Use the reflection and rehearsal process to improve your final scene?		
Personal Goal #1:		
Personal Goal #2:		
Final Score (out of 100):		

It is also useful to schedule the project in its entirety and to write the project dates into the planning sheet (page 131).

Step Three: Introduce the Project to the Students

Say,

In social studies, you have been studying the turn of the twentieth century. As you know, this was a period of time that had many changes in it, especially in America. We are going to create a living newspaper about this topic. A living newspaper is a drama technique developed during the Depression to quickly share information with an audience, especially with audiences that lived in rural areas where few people may have been taught to read well. A living newspaper is like a regular newspaper because it is made up of several stories, and each story is about something different. But it is different because instead of being a written project, your story will be acted out.

We are going to divide you randomly into groups of four to five students. Each group will choose from the topics listed on this sheet, or, if you have an idea that is not listed here, you may suggest one to us. You will research the topic and work with members of your group to create a dramatic scene that describes it. A "scene" is a smaller part of a play. Scenes have beginnings, middles, and ends. The groups can use any of the techniques we've explored earlier: tableau, narrative pantomime, even a monologue, like we used for the wax museum. You may use costumes, props, or basic set pieces, but remember to keep these simple, because during the performance we will move quickly from one skit to the next, with little time for setting up.

This means that your research must have a focus: you don't need to tell us *everything* about your topic. Your goal is to tell us a *story* about your topic in a way that will make the audience want to ask questions and learn more about it. Choose your facts wisely–not everything you read belongs in your dramatic story. Real reporters have stories that answer these questions: Who? What? When? Where? Why? How? Use those questions to guide your research and writing. They will help your story be more detailed and lively.

The groups will act like reporters. But just like real newspaper reporters, you will have editors—your classroom teacher and me—to help guide you in your work, help you do your best, and assemble the final "stories" in a meaningful order. In a real newspaper, the editors observe the work of the reporters. They give help reporters need it, and when the paper is about to be printed, the editors have the final word on the order in which the stories go. We, your instructors, will do the same for you—we will help you when you ask for help or when we sense that you need it, and we will help the class place the scenes in a sequence.

All newspaper articles have a headline, a few words that tell readers what the story they are about to read is about. Your scene will also have a headline. Your group will create a short phrase and say it aloud together to start and end the scene.

Here is the rubric (*distribute form from page 128*) that we will use to evaluate your work. Like other rubrics we've done before, this rubric has a column where you evaluate your own work, and a column where your instructors will evaluate your work. Take a look at the last two rows on the rubric. Notice how they say "Personal Goal." Before you even begin working on this project, we want you to think about the projects you've done in the past. Each of you has some areas of strength, and each of you has something you may be working on, like speaking more loudly or using your body to communicate more effectively, finding the main idea in research, even writing skills like capitalizing and punctuating. Think about two personal goals you'd like to set for yourself for this project and fill them in there. You'll discuss your goals with your instructors during the first conference. Be sure to read through the rubric and ask us questions before you start working as a group.

Twice during this project, your instructors will conference with you. A conference is a quick meeting where we find out what progress you've made and what you plan to do next. The conferences help keep you on top of your work and help us know where we can assist you.

Another tool we'll use to stay focused on our work are project folders (*pass them out*) and planning sheets (*pass out form from page 131, with deadlines filled in by the instructors in advance*). Keep all of your work, including the rubric, in the project folder. In your first meeting with your group, please fill in the planning sheet. Use pencil, as things may change as you work through the project.

Now, we're going to divide you into groups. In this jar, we've put each of your names on a piece of paper. We'll draw the names randomly to keep things fair. (*Teachers draw names to select groups.*)

Now, find the other members of your group. Choose a topic from the list, and begin brainstorming. When there are ten minutes left in class, we'll ask you to begin filling in the planning sheet. Tomorrow, we'll begin conferencing with the groups to see what you've chosen."

Planning Sheet: Living Newspaper

Name _____

Other Students in Group: _____

_____

Project Type (check one):
[ ] Tableau   [ ] Narrative Pantomime
[ ] Monologue(s)   [ ] Other: _____
[ ] Drama Machine

Roles in Our Scene:

Role   Played by
_____

_____

_____

_____

_____

_____

--continue on back side of paper if needed--

We will need these props, costumes, and other items:

Item   Will be brought/made by:
_____

_____

_____

_____

_____

_____

--continue on back side of paper if needed--

Initial Research Questions (What do we need to find out first in our research?)

Important Dates:

Project Assigned:	_____	Class Rehearsals:	_____
Conference #1:	_____	Performance Date:	_____
In-Class Research Dates:	_____	Folder & Rubric Due:	_____
Outline or script due:	_____		
Conference #2:	_____		

Step Four: Research

Once groups have selected their topics, they are ready to conduct research. As they research, continue to help them make the connection between what they are reading online or in print and the dramatic story they will be assembling. Probing questions from the media specialist can help students focus their scene and their research time. For example, these nonjudgmental questions might help guide students while keeping students as the decision makers: "It sounds like you are interested in the Wright Brothers' childhood years. How will that improve your scene, which you told me will be about the first flight at Kitty Hawk?" or, "I like the idea of making a fashion scene about Gibson Girls and their fashions. You have a lot of research here about men's fashions, too. Will your scene be about men's fashions, too, or just about women's fashions?"

Planning Sheets and Project Folders

The planning sheet mentioned in Step Three (page 131) helps students envision the project and provides structure for group work. Ask each student to keep an individual project folder and planning sheet. Collect the folders at the end of each work session so nothing gets misplaced. For dedicated students who want to continue to work outside of school, offer to make a photocopy and keep the original in the folder.

▶ Printouts/Photocopies of Research

As in any research project that asks students to create their own product, comprehension errors can lead to mistaken assumptions. It can be useful, especially with Web-based research, to ask students to make a printout or photocopy of research. Keep highlighters available for student use and instruct them in efficient note taking using a highlighter and a pencil to take notes in the margins. This avoids the lengthy process of using note cards, which can demotivate students, and better replicates real-world research among adults. When a group gets stuck during the creation process, or if a suspicious fact arises, students and teachers can move quickly to the printout to track down more information or the source of the questionable information, without need for Internet access.

▶ Conferencing

Especially with fifth and sixth graders, a group conference with the teacher can help students move from research to action. Consider scheduling a conference with each group once the planning sheet has been filled out and again after an outline (for improvised projects like a tableau) or script has been created. The goals of a conference are to discuss what has been learned, what is still unknown, the best search strategies for finding the information (print or image databases, the surface web, encyclopedias, person-to-person interviews, etc.), and the timeline for the work.

Step Five: Writing and Preparing

The collaborating teachers' objectives for the unit should specify whether or not a formal script is required. If a formally written script is required (which means that improvised activities such as a drama machine or tableau may not be options), it should be structured according to the school district's approved writing process. However, for some scenes, a simple outline of ideas or a sequence of steps may be sufficient.

Step Six: Small Group Rehearsals and Self-Evaluation

When the script or outline is complete, the groups are ready to begin rehearsals. One common pitfall in small groups is that they spend the bulk of their time standing in place and discussing what they *will* do instead of *doing* it! While some discussion is important in all theatrical endeavors, so is the physical practice. Begin rehearsals with the Welcoming Ritual and a few warm-up activities to prepare students for movement.

During rehearsals, the instructional team rotates between groups to keep the students on task, pointing out positive achievements and offering constructive comments.

Sometimes it is not until students get on their feet and rehearse that they realize they need more information than originally planned. This is a real-world teachable moment because it reflects the research process used by adults, who gather information, stop when they think they have enough, start making the work product, and then realize that the gathered information is insufficient. Encourage students who suddenly find their content to be insubstantial to return to their research tools, either by rereading their notated printouts or by returning to print or online resources for additional information. Avoid the trap of "punishing" students in this situation by saying, "You've had three days to research. Now you'll have to go with what you have," as this ultimately encourages children to be satisfied with incomplete research. Find time for those students to revisit the research process.

When the students have had a chance to rehearse, provide an opportunity to reflect and self-evaluate. Because students have been given the choice of format —narrative pantomime, tableau, or wax museum—refer to those chapters for sample handouts, or distribute the list of questions in the handout on page 134 for students' responses.

Student Reflection:
Living Newspaper Rehearsal

Name:

_____

Now that you have completed your Living Newspaper rehearsal, take a moment to reflect on how you are doing so far. Write your answers below.

1. Do we have enough historical information to make an interesting scene?

2. Is our scene both entertaining and factual?

3. Can we be heard?

4. Are we using interesting voices?

5. Do we have body language, levels, and gestures that help to tell the story?

6. Is our group communicating well and demonstrating good teamwork?

7. Am I communicating well and being a good team player?

8. What is one thing I could do to improve this performance?

9. What is one thing I am doing well and should keep doing?

10. What is one word I could use to describe how we are doing so far?

11. What do I need from my teachers in order to create an outstanding scene?

Step Seven: Previewing and Sequencing Scenes

The goal for this session is for each group to see the other scenes and to sequence them. Begin with some warm-ups from chapter 2, being sure to select some that warm up both the body and the voice.

Next, invite each group to perform its scene once for the rest of the class. The goal of this presentation is for students to become familiar with the work of others. Often students find connections between each others' work, and their recognition of these connections is part of what helps them create a more holistic and deeper understanding of the historical period.

Another goal for this first presentation is to help nervous students relax. It is much easier to present in front of classmates before presenting to an outside audience. Similarly, this rehearsal time helps students get out their giggles so they can concentrate more seriously during the actual performance.

When all groups have finished staging their scenes, invite the class to assist in sequencing the scenes into an appropriate order for performance. Notice that there is no feedback session during this rehearsal. The goal of the presentations is to see the content so it can be sequenced. Letting the class know in advance that this will not be a feedback session may soothe some nervous students.

Through observation, it will be clear that some groups are stronger or weaker than others. Place these scenes appropriately in the living newspaper sequence. For example, a superior group should not be placed too early in the performance, as it will overshadow the others and make the remainder of the production feel anticlimactic. Similarly, if one group is clearly the weakest, try to place it earlier so it does not weaken the finale.

Step Eight: Whole Class Runthroughs

"Runthrough" means a rehearsal of a play in which all scenes are rehearsed in order, preferably without stopping. When doing runthroughs with an entire class, it is important to work quickly and efficiently. With a living newspaper runthrough, you may be working with four or five students at a time, which means that 20 or 25 are *not* working and will be tempted to chat or lose their focus. Unless there is an emergency, try to let the whole sequence run without interrupting for comments. Use a clipboard to take notes instead and hold your feedback until the end.

If this is a team-taught project, consider splitting the class in half, with one-half rehearsing with one instructor while the other instructor leads the other half in a different activity.

Step Nine: Feedback and Reflection

Several techniques for feedback can be effective at this step:

> • **Public self-evaluation:** The instructors may ask a group to reflect on its own performance before asking the "audience" for feedback. Say to the group members, "Why don't you start us off? What did you see as your own strengths? Weaknesses? What will you keep? What will you be working on?" This encourages self-reflection and not just, "We're fixing it because the teacher told us to."

- **"Sandwiching":** This feedback technique, described in greater detail in chapter 5, structures class feedback by asking for positive comments first, then moving to constructive criticism, then ending with a reminder of the best things that should not be changed. The goal is to emphasize the positive.

- **Videotaping and using the four-square evaluation sheet:** Another important reflection tool can be videotaping a runthrough. Before students view the video, distribute the four-square performance reflection sheet (page 114) and ask students to fill it out privately. Sometimes this form of silent evaluation is as effective as discussion.

Step Ten: Invite an Audience

▶ *Live Audience*

Because the entire class is involved in the living newspaper, it needs an audience that can appreciate its work. As is described in more detail in chapter 4, invite your teaching colleagues to bring their classes to witness the living newspaper and enlist the student actors, possibly in partnership with the art teacher, to make publicity posters. Be sure to do this one week or more prior to the performance so teachers have time to adjust their lesson plans.

▶ *Morning News Broadcast*

Though a live audience is best for a live theatrical performance because the performers get direct feedback from the audience, a video performance is the next best thing. Many schools have a morning broadcast. Since most living newspapers last 10 minutes or less, they may be suitable for broadcast during morning announcements.

Step Eleven: Performance.

Prior to the performance, the class should engage in a few warm-up activities to prepare the body and voice. The performance should begin with a welcome from a student or one of the instructors that provides a general overview of the learning objectives and drama techniques used in the performance. Then let the students run the performance while the instructors stand in the back. Keep rubrics (page 128) at hand for comments, though by this point the instructors will be familiar with each group's work. Afterward, a student or instructor should thank the classes for coming.

Step Twelve: Reflection

After the performance, thank the student performers for their hard work. Ask if the cast has any additional comments they would like to share. Pass out the rubrics when they are completed.

■ CONCLUSION

A living newspaper is both homage to a creative Depression-era project and a way to assemble several small group projects into a meaningful whole. Because student groups must process and distill research into a creative product, it is virtually plagiarism proof. The performance aspect increases a student's motivation to do great work.

■ REFERENCES

Bentley, Joanne. 1988. *Hallie Flanagan: A Life in the American Theatre.* New York: Alfred A. Knopf. 436pp. ISBN 0394570413.

Flanagan, Hallie. 1940. *Arena: The Story of the Federal Theatre.* New York: Limelight Editions, 475pp. ISBN 0879100338 pbk.

McMaster, Jennifer Catney. 1998. " 'Doing' Literature: Using Drama to Build Literacy." *The Reading Teacher* 51(7): 574–584.

Part II
Working with the Voice

Chapter 8
Oral Tapestries: Choral Readings (Grades 2 and Up)

■ INTRODUCTION

Part II focuses on the voice and vocal projects that can be used in media center lessons. "Spoken word" activities are oral projects that rely on the voice and are powerful ways of getting students engaged in and motivated about their learning.

The focus of this chapter is choral readings. For the purposes of this chapter, a choral reading can be any piece of text that is spoken aloud by a group of people. Choral readings occur when a poem or other text is divided up into "parts." Various class members take on the "parts." The result is a richly textured reading.

Choral work has its roots in ancient Greek plays, in which there were few solo actors but a large chorus. The chorus was a collection of people who chanted responses to the situations of the main characters. Today, choral readings do not require chanting, nor do they require that everyone speak simultaneously.

Choral readings can be found in existing published works, or they can be custom-made by instructors based on existing poems and texts. This chapter will explore many options for choral readings. Please note that some of the activities in this chapter involve making photocopies of poems or making transparencies to put an on overhead projector. Most materials are available for fair use in educational settings, but please consult your district's copyright policies if these works will be publicly performed or recorded outside an educational setting.

These readings can be used as stand-alone activities for literature appreciation (such as a reading of a seasonal Jack Prelutsky poem) or to make deep and meaningful connections to the curriculum. For example, students can examine the text of Dr. Martin Luther King Jr.'s "I have a dream" speech through choral reading and come away with a greater understanding of King's message. Choral readings are a natural fit for National Poetry Month in April or a language arts poetry unit.

Benefits of Choral Readings

Choral readings help students break down a larger text into smaller, more digestible pieces. Because each student is focusing on just a few phrases, comprehension increases. Asking students to make deliberate vocal choices requires a close reading of the text, another tool that strengthens comprehension. Weaker readers benefit from hearing text read aloud by others. Text mastery occurs phrase by phrase, not page by page, helping to scaffold comprehension of more difficult texts. The activity brings poetry alive, allowing students to hear consonance, assonance, and rhythmic patterns. Choral readings are collaborative and collective in nature and allow active students to *talk* while learning! At the same time, participants speak up only at a predetermined time. This promotes self-control and teamwork. As students rehearse and repeat a choral reading activity, comprehension deepens.

Finding a Choral Reading

There are several ways to obtain choral readings. First, choral readings can be taken from an existing book of poems for multiple voices. Second, the class can be divided in half and alternate lines or stanzas in a poem. Next, in collaboration with the classroom teacher, a curriculum-related poem or text can be divided into two or more parts. To emphasize the meaning of the text, vary the number of students speaking at once or overlap the parts. Finally, a spontaneous choral reading can occur when an instructor reads a text aloud and students choose when to join the reading. Each method is explored in this chapter. A lesson plan for how to conducting choral readings concludes the chapter.

■ WARMING UP

As with drama activities, it is recommended that choral reading main lessons be preceded by a Welcoming Ritual and a series of vocal warm-ups. These are available in chapter 2.

■ USING BOOKS WRITTEN FOR MULTIPLE VOICES

Some books are already divided into multiple voices. These make an easy entry into choral readings with students. Project the book pages onto the wall or screen so they are a size that can be seen by the entire class. Some books for multiple voices use color coding to identify parts. An opaque projector or document camera is ideal for projecting full-color images. Split the class in half, with a small aisle separating the groups to prevent confusion among weak readers. For very young students, the media specialist can stand in front of the students, swaying slightly to one side as he or she reads along with the entire group. After reading the poem through once or twice to decode text and discuss comprehension concerns, work on building vocal variety using the techniques featured later in this chapter.

Books Written for Multiple Voices

Fleischman, Paul. *Big Talk: Poems for Four Voices.* 1st ed. Illustrated by Beppe Giacobbe. Cambridge, MA: Candlewick, 2000. 44pp. ISBN 0763606367.

Fleischman, Paul. *I Am Phoenix: Poems for Two Voices.* 1st ed. New York: Harper & Row, 1985. 51pp. ISBN 0060218819; 0060218827 (lib. bdg.).

Fleischman, Paul. *Joyful Noise: Poems for Two Voices.* 1st ed. Illustrated by Eric Bedews. New York: Harper & Row, 1988. 44pp. ISBN 0060218525; 0060218533 (lib. bdg.); 0064460932 (pbk.).

Harrison, David L. *Farmer's Dog Goes to the Forest: Rhymes for Two Voices.* 1st ed. Illustrated by Arden Johnson-Petrov. Honesdale, PA: Wordsong/Boyds Mill Press, 2005. 29pp. ISBN 1590782429.

Harrison, David L. *Farmer's Garden: Rhymes for Two Voices.* 1st ed. Illustrated by Arden Johnson-Petrov. Honesdale, PA: Wordsong/Boyds Mill Press, 2000. unpaged. ISBN 1563977761.

Hoberman, Mary Ann. *Very Short Stories to Read Together.* 1st ed. Illustrated by Michael Emberley. New York: Little, Brown, 2001. unpaged. ISBN 0316363502.

Hoberman, Mary Ann. *You Read to Me, I'll Read to You: Very Short Fairy Tales to Read Together (in Which Wolves Are Tamed, Trolls Are Transformed, and Peas Are Triumphant).* 1st ed. Illustrated by Michael Emberley. New York: Little, Brown, 2004. 32pp. ISBN 0316146110.

Hoberman, Mary Ann. *You Read to Me, I'll Read to You: Very Short Mother Goose Tales to Read Together.* 1st ed. Illustrated by Michael Emberley. New York: Little, Brown, 2005. 32pp. ISBN 0316144312.

■ ALTERNATING LINES OR STANZAS

If a text is not already divided into parts, your students can divide it into parts "on the go." Divide the class into two groups for the first effort; later, the class can divide into more groups for more complex poems. Ask students to make a small aisle to separate the two groups.

Copy the poem onto a transparency. Number each line by placing the number to the left of each line. Assign one group to read the odd-numbered lines (e.g., lines 1, 3, and 5) and another to read the even-numbered lines (2, 4, 6, etc.). Another option is for one group to read the first stanza (a stanza is like a "paragraph" of a poem; stanzas are separated on the page by a blank line), the second group the second stanza, and so on. Dividing the class in half by gender or alphabetically by last name is an alternative to quickly divide into groups.

As an alternative to numbering, delineate parts by underlining text in different colors using a washable transparency marker.

■ INSTRUCTOR-CREATED CHORAL READINGS

It is easy to create a choral reading from an existing poem. These choral readings are not only useful as stand-alone projects but can also provide scripts for shadow puppet plays, radio plays, or readers' theatre scripts. To create a choral reading, follow the steps discussed below.

Work in collaboration with the classroom teacher to select a text. For the purposes of example here, the classroom teacher is introducing a fourth-grade unit on immigration, and the media specialist will lead a choral reading with an excerpt from the Emma Lazarus poem, "The New Colossus," which is affixed to the base of the Statue of Liberty. This will become a jumping-off point for further discussion on nineteenth-century American attitudes about immigration.

Decide on the number of groups. There can be as few as two groups and as many as the number of students in the class. If this is a class's first time doing a choral reading, try using just two groups until they get used to the format. Students' independent reading ability is the guideline for the number of groups into which you will divide the class. Emergent readers can often barely read ahead, so keeping them in just two parts makes sense. Generally, second graders can have two groups, third grade up to four groups, and fourth graders have developed the ability to "read ahead" well enough for each class member to have his or her own part. For the Lazarus example, four groups are used.

Type the text in paragraph form into a word processing program. For the Emma Lazarus poem, the entire text is as follows:

The New Colossus
Emma Lazarus

Not like the brazen giant of Greek fame,
With conquering limbs astride from land to land;
Here at our sea-washed, sunset gates shall stand
A mighty woman with a torch, whose flame
Is the imprisoned lightning, and her name Mother of Exiles.
From her beacon-hand
Glows world-wide welcome; her mild eyes command
The air-bridged harbor that twin cities frame.
"Keep, ancient lands, your storied pomp!" cries she
With silent lips. "Give me your tired, your poor,
Your huddled masses yearning to breathe free,
The wretched refuse of your teeming shore.
Send these, the homeless, tempest-tost to me,
I lift my lamp beside the golden door!"

Next, chop the text up into phrases. Each group should receive at least one phrase. A group might receive an entire sentence or just a phrase. With poetry, an idea sometimes begins on one line but continues onto the next. For choral readings, you can sometimes ignore line breaks (the point in a line of text where the "return key" was pressed and a new line was started) and, instead, divide up phrases according to their meaning. This step is particularly important for elementary students who need the comprehension assistance.

To indicate parts, assign a distinctive font to each group. The choral reading will now look like the example on page 146.

Notice how, for comprehension's sake, some text that was originally on two lines has been moved to a single line. This makes the words flow naturally and makes it easier for students to read.

Does it seem that this text is too complex for a fourth-grade class? The great strategy of this technique is that by breaking phrases down into small but decipherable chunks and removing line breaks that are poetically beautiful but obscure meaning, students' comprehension will actually go up, making primary source or historical text more accessible and understandable. There may be a few words or ideas, such as the Greek statue or "exiles" or "storied pomp" that need some prereading definitions, but it is amazing what the students will be able to understand.

If working with ESL or below-grade-level readers, consider condensing the text being studied, instead beginning this exercise at the famous line, "Bring me your tired."

Adding Texture and Layers

While simply having groups alternate is a quick and easy way to make a choral reading, far more poignant, touching, or powerful effects can be created when the number of voices ebbs and flows, text overlaps, and more than one group speaks at once.

For this technique to work, simply marking the text in different fonts will not work. In this example, it will be important to create two columns. In the left column should be a notation of who will speak, and in the second column goes the text. Each student is assigned a number.

The New Colossus

Emma Lazarus

Name _____

You are in Group _____

A choral reading in four parts

Group 1

Group 2

Group 3

Group 4

Not like the brazen giant of Greek fame,

With conquering limbs astride from land to land;

Here at our sea-washed, sunset gates shall stand

A mighty woman with a torch,

whose flame is the imprisoned lightning,

and her name Mother of Exiles.

From her beacon-hand glows world-wide welcome;

her mild eyes command the air-bridged harbor that twin cities frame.

"Keep, ancient lands, your storied pomp!" cries she with silent lips.

"Give me your tired,

your poor,

Your huddled masses yearning to breathe free,

The wretched refuse of your teeming shore.

Send these,

the homeless,

tempest-tost to me,

I lift my lamp beside the golden door!"

Sometimes a number speaks alone, but students may be clustered into groups, such as "1–15," "odds," "evens," "girls," "boys," or "ALL." Varying the number of students speaking at once adds gentle rising and falling to the vocal presentation, with emphasis on the most important phrases. A line delivered solely by girls will have a different vocal tone from a line spoken by boys.

This assignment technique allows us to assign more than one group to read a given line. There may be words that are so important in the text that they should be said by more than one group. For example, in the Lazarus poem, the opening words, "Give me," are so important that they might be said by the entire class, which would be noted as "ALL" in the margin. Similarly, the phrase, "yearning to breathe free" might need two or three groups. There might even be a phrase for which having a single voice might add poignancy. For example, "your poor" might be heart-wrenching if said by a single, small voice. In this case, mark a specific child's name in the margin, like, "JENNIFER."

Give students a moment to mark their parts with a highlighter or colored pencil before beginning. This technique requires a few more rehearsals but is wondrously resonant to hear, especially when the refinements in the next section are applied.

When Lazarus's poem is reedited to include all of these ideas and divided into 24 unique parts, one for every student (if there are more than 24 students, ask two children to double up on the same number), the result is as shown on page 148.

The New Colossus

Emma Lazarus

Name _____

You are part number _____

A choral reading in twenty-four parts

1 & 2:	Not like the
1, 2, 3, 4:	brazen giant
1& 2:	of Greek fame,
5 & 6:	With conquering limbs astride from land to land;
7 & 8:	Here at our
7, 8, 9, 10:	sea-washed, sunset gates
9 & 10:	shall stand
GIRLS:	A mighty woman with a torch,
BOYS:	whose flame is the imprisoned lightning,
11 & 12:	and her name?
ALL:	Mother of Exiles.
13 & 14:	From her beacon-hand
13, 14, 15, 16:	glows world-wide welcome.
17 & 18:	Her mild eyes
17, 18, 19, 20:	command
19, 20:	the air-bridged harbor that twin cities frame.
21, 22, 23, 24:	"Keep, ancient lands, your storied pomp!" cries she with silent lips.
ALL:	"Give me your tired,
JENNIFER:	your poor,
1 & 2:	Your huddled masses
GIRLS:	yearning
EVEN GIRLS:	to breathe free,
ODDS:	The wretched refuse of your teeming shore.
EVEN BOYS:	Send these, the homeless, tempest-tost to me.
ALL:	I lift my lamp beside the golden door!"

■ SPONTANEOUS CHORAL READINGS

On-the-fly choral readings are created spontaneously in the classroom, with no predefined parts. Students select and speak the text they feel is most meaningful. For this technique, each student will need a copy of the text and a pencil or highlighter.

Say to the students,

> Today, we are going to create a choral reading. A choral reading is a poem or a piece of writing that is read aloud by an entire group. Sometimes just one person speaks, sometimes a few people speak, and sometimes everyone speaks.
>
> We're going to create the choral reading ourselves. I'll start by reading the poem aloud. Whenever I read something that you think is interesting or beautiful or meaningful or important, highlight or underline those words or phrases. You might underline something because it makes you think of a memory or because you like the sound of the words or because you think the author picked a perfect adjective or word.

During the reading, walk around the room to monitor student progress and understanding of the assignment. At the conclusion, say, "Has everyone marked at least one thing?" If a student confesses to a blank page, say, "Right now, pick at least one thing to mark."

Say,

> Now I am going to read it again. This time, when I get to something you've highlighted, join in with me and speak your highlighted text aloud with me. Stop speaking when you get to the end of the text you highlighted.

Read the text again and enjoy the coming and going of voices. Sometimes the instructor's voice is the only one speaking. Sometimes just a few voices speak up, and sometimes every voice chimes in. Lead a brief discussion about why there might have been some phrases that everyone said (possible answers: they are the most beautiful/descriptive/important phrases) and why there were some phrases repeated by few (ideas seemed important, vivid image, text-to-self connection, etc.).

Texts That Adapt Well into Choral Readings

Patriotic and historic texts, including the Preamble to the Constitution, the Declaration of Independence, the Gettysburg Address, Martin Luther King's "I have a dream" speech, or Sojourner Truth's "Ain't I a woman?" have complex sentence structure and meaning. Choral readings help students digest these difficult texts. In addition, these texts also have metaphorical meaning that can ignite creative vocal interpretations

Children's poetry books such as those by Douglas Florian, Jack Prelutsky, and Shel Silverstein provide entertaining poems. Harlem Renaissance poetry by Langston Hughes or James Weldon Johnson connects history to literature.

Lyrical or mysterious passages in chapter books are another source of choral readings. Excerpt a suspenseful passage from a ghost story or mystery and invite students to make a choral reading so scary the hair stands up on their arms. Create a choral reading from the opening words of a chapter book to explore how the author sets context. Ask students to identify the climactic moment or a moment when a character makes an important discovery or has a revelation. Show the impact of that moment through a choral reading.

Whatever text is chosen, consider folding the following performance strategies into the lesson in order to integrate the arts into the experience.

■ ADDING VOCAL TECHNIQUE TO A CHORAL READING

This section of the chapter provides drama strategies for breathing life into a choral reading. These strategies help move the class in the direction of *art*, not simply recitation. By being asked to make an *artistic interpretation* of a text, students are called upon to think deeply about meaning and how to express that meaning. Those are the activities that deepen comprehension and solidify the text's meaning in the student's mind. The following lesson plan structure can help develop the artistry of a choral reading.

- **When working with choral text, read through it more than once.** The first time through, students will be concentrating more on decoding and comprehension. After the first time, encourage vocal variety. Using the vocal skills outlined in chapter 2—pitch, volume, speed, and tone/energy—demonstrate how making the voice louder or softer, faster or slower, or deeper or higher; using sharp or honeyed-tones; or speaking sincerely or with affectation can do so much to make a text come vividly alive. A good choral reading should be rehearsed at least three times: once for decoding, once to attempt vocal variety, and once to refine the performance. Build in time for feedback and reflection.

- **Experiment with different vocal styles as a class to show how these deliveries change the meaning for the reader.** How is the text different if read to sound joyful? Sad? Frustrated? Angry? Frightened? What if it were read in the monotonous tone of a broadcaster? Performed as if the students are sportscasters at an exciting event? What if the poem had to be read in its entirety in 30 seconds to avert nuclear disaster? How would a mother read this poem to a baby? If the students were trying to whisper this poem to each other during a test without being caught, how would they read? What if they were reading it to someone who is hard of hearing? How could they read the text like a love letter? Like hate mail? Like a good or bad report card? From these exercises, students will discover a meaningful and successful method of delivery.

- If the choral reading is being performed by groups and the text is divided by line or stanza (no overlaps), let **each group work independently** to come up with a way of delivering the text that is interesting.

- Ask students, **"Which words are the most important in your phrase? Should they get more emphasis or less?"** Withdrawing vocal energy can be as effective as adding it. (Ask your students how they know their parents are really, really mad. Is it when their parents' voices become very, very *quiet*? Ask students to circle or highlight the key words in their lines. These are the words where vocal variety choices need to be made.

- **Point out how punctuation marks like question or exclamation marks give hints to the readers how to perform.** Question marks should cause the voice to rise at the end of the sentence. Exclamation points indicate an elevation in energy: surprise, excitement, or shock.

These techniques will do much to infuse the projects with artistry. While a choral reading can be a nonassessed introductory activity, if it is used as a main lesson, the rubric on page 152 could be used.

Name _____

Class _____

Assessment Rubric – Choral Reading

Key:	
+	Exceeded expectations
✓	Met expectations
-	Did not meet expectations

Did you . . .	Self-Evaluation	Teacher Evaluation
Participate actively in the lesson?		
Make a good effort?		
Respect the work of your colleagues?		
Make appropriate vocal choices?		
Contribute to classroom discussions and plans?		
Restate the meaning of the text in your own words?		

■ Conclusion

Choral readings are wonderful ways to explore the meaning of poems, descriptive texts, and historical writings. The close attention played to specific words, their meanings, and how they can be delivered with maximum effect raises comprehension, while students remain motivated to do great work.

■ Additional Reading

Read Write Think. *Multipurpose Poetry: Introducing Science Concepts and Increasing Fluency.* Available at http://www.readwritethink.org/lessons/lesson_view.asp?id=69 (accessed August 21, 2006).

Chapter 9

Drama on the Air: Using Podcasting to Create Radio Plays (Grades 3 and Up)

■ INTRODUCTION

When I was in first grade, my teacher set up a recording studio in the corner of our classroom near the sink. Each week, we would visit the tape recorder and record our thoughts. I still remember how I signed off at the end of each of my recordings: "This is Kristin Fontichiaro in Room 102." It was so exhilarating and motivating! Why stop at a few terse sentences when we could say everything that was on our minds? Speaking into the tape recorder was more intimate and less intimidating than speaking in front of the class.

That memory came flooding back when I first heard about podcasting. Podcasting is a growing trend in which audiorecordings are made using an inexpensive microphone and free or inexpensive computer software. "Digital audio" is another term that can be used instead of podcasting. The term "podcast" is a combination of the word "broadcast" with "iPod," but iPods or mp3 players are not a necessity.

Unlike cassette recordings, podcasts can easily be edited. Recordings can be made on multiple tracks, making it easy to add sound effects or music after the spoken recording is completed. Students' work can be distributed quickly and at little or no cost. It can be sent as an e-mail attachment, downloaded to an iPod or mp3 player, posted to a Web site or blog, even automatically downloaded to patrons' iTunes if set up with a Real Simple Syndication (RSS) feed. This makes it easy to share student work with colleagues, other classrooms, parents, relatives, and community stakeholders. The glamour of recording oneself and having others hear can be intoxicating, and so it is a learning path many students will be eager to pursue.

Digital audiorecordings provide a fast way to capture and document student learning. Unlike digital movies, which require hours of editing, a digital recording can be made and edited in minutes and be online or burned to CD within 30 minutes. It is especially useful for students with special needs who might have great ideas but difficulty transcribing them in written form. For those students with creative minds but learning disabilities, digital audio may be the perfect means to show off their talents without struggling to put pencil to paper.

This chapter looks at how podcasting can be used in combination with drama techniques to create a radio play. Before examining this project, a review of the necessary equipment is in order.

▪ PODCASTING EQUIPMENT

Podcasting requires very little equipment: a computer, microphones, and software.

Computer

Podcasts can be made on both Macintosh and Windows platforms. The open-source software Audacity, which is used as the model software for this chapter, works on both platforms, extending as far back as the Mac OS9 and Windows 98 platforms. Either a desktop or a laptop will work, though a laptop's portability makes it easy for the technology to travel.

Selecting a Microphone

The type of microphone depends on the ports available on the host computer. To podcast, the computer must have both an *input* and an *output* jack. An *input* jack receives the sound from the microphone. On a PC or older Macintosh computer, this will be a small round jack with a microphone icon. An *output* jack sends the recorded sound out through headphones. The output jack is another small, round jack labeled with a headphones icon.

If both of these small round jacks are present, students can use a headphone with a built-in microphone (it will look something like a stripped-down pilot's or operator's headset), as seen in this photo.

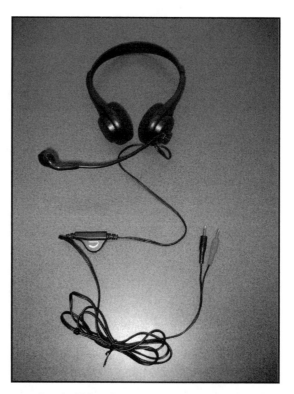

This inexpensive Avid headset makes crisp and clear recordings.

For two-person projects, consider purchasing a pair of Y-adapters from a stereo equipment store. These adapters will allow two headphones to be plugged into the headphone jack and two microphones into the microphone jack. If a project requires more than two students to speak, gang headphones together with additional adapters. Up to four sets of headsets can be ganged together with little or no impact on recording quality.

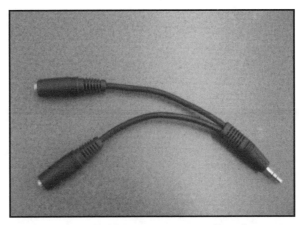

Y-adapters are available at stereo stores. Purchase two: one for the microphone input and one for the headphone jack.

Newer Macintosh computers may not have microphone jacks. In that case, consider a USB microphone. These microphones range in price from $40 to over $150. Most have a built-in stand for tabletop use. The person speaking must move quite close to the microphone to get a clear sound. USB microphones are also good when several voices speak at once. Some newer laptop computers have built-in microphones with remarkably good sound quality.

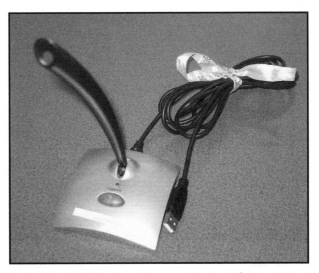

This Logitech USB microphone costs about $40 retail and is appropriate for computers that lack a standard microphone jack or for recording sound effects.

Downloading the Software

There are many software options for recording digital audio, including Garage Band and QuickTime Pro. New Macintosh computers ship with the iLife multimedia suite, which includes the audio software Garage Band. However, this chapter focuses on Audacity, an open-source software available for free download (http://audacity.sourceforge.net). When downloading, choose the version that matches your operating system. Follow the online instructions for downloading Audacity and LAME, a small file that works with Audacity to convert the raw Audacity work files into the mp3 format that is compatible with mp3 players and can also be read by iTunes and other media players. The LAME file can be hidden anywhere. The first time the FILE > EXPORT TO MP3 option is activated, the user is asked to navigate to the saved LAME file. After this first use, Audacity remembers where LAME is stored and does not prompt the user again.

Next, download iTunes, Apple's free multimedia management software (http://www.apple.com/itunes). This is available for Mac OS X or Windows operating systems. iTunes helps organize audio files, burn CDs, and transfer files to an iPod device. (Note that the iPod line of products is the only brand of mp3 players compatible with iTunes as of the writing of this book. iPods manufactured after September 2006 may require the use of a computer with higher-speed USB 2.0 ports. Consult the online technical specifications at http://www.apple.com/ipod.)

When the equipment is assembled and the software is downloaded, the computer is ready to record and distribute a radio play. Details about using Audacity are available on page 159.

Making a Podcast with Audacity

1. Prepare for the recording session. Plug in the microphone. If it has an on/off switch, turn it on. If there is a volume control, turn it all the way up. Turn on the computer and open the Audacity software. Set scripts down on the table to avoid rustling noises during the recording session. Take a deep breath and get ready to record.

2. Record. When ready, click on the red "RECORD" button on the top menu and begin to speak. Notice the blue sound wave pattern appearing midway down the screen. If it is a flat line, it is not picking up any sound. When it is picking up sound, blue sound waves will appear. Try to speak loudly enough (or put the microphone closer to your mouth) so that the blue waves fill up about half of the recording bar. The first time you use Audacity, you may wish to record just the opening words of your project to test the sound levels. Click the STOP button on the top menu when you have finished recording.

3. Review what has been recorded. Click the REWIND button (two triangles pointing left). If the recording sound good, continue with the next step. If not, go to FILE > NEW and start over again.

4. Edit out "blank air" moments, where the blue sound wave appears horizontal. Highlight the part you want to delete. Then click EDIT > CUT.

5. Add music or record a sound effects track. Creativecommons.org has a searchable list of music that can be downloaded and used wihtout charge for educational or podcasting projects. To add downloaded music, go to PROJECT > IMPORT AUDIO and navigate to the music file. Make creative sound effects from scraps of wood, musical instruments, noisemakers, or toys. Record sound effects on a separate track from the spoken word track to facilitate editing. To do this, set Audacity to play back the first track when adding a second. Go to FILE > PREFERENCES > AUDIO I/O , check "Play other tracks while recording," and click OK. After the speaking parts are recorded, click the REWIND button (two left-pointing triangles). Then push RECORD. A new track will appear under the speech track. The recorded text will be heard so that the sound effects can be placed in precisely the right spot. If corrections need to be made, just record the affected track rather than starting from scratch.

6. Save project and export as an mp3 file. Audacity saves its files in its own unique file format. Use FILE > SAVE PROJECT to save large projects periodically. To be used for burning a CD, importing to iTunes, emailing, or posting online, the file must then be exported into mp3 format. Go to FILE > EXPORT AS MP3 and decide where to save it and what file name to give it. Click SAVE. The first time an mp3 is made, Audacity will prompt the user to identify where the LAME converter is stored. See the downloading instructions at http://audacity.sourceforge.net for details.

7. Add metadata to the file. Metadata is a collection of words that describe the audio file. Metadata is useful when your file is imported into iTunes; it will be the information that appears about your file (the document name assigned in Step 6 will not appear). A dialog box will pop up asking for some information. For TITLE, give the name of the student's work (i.e., "Pioneer radio play"). For ARTIST, give just a first name, class ("third grade") or even a student number. Don't use specific names that you don't want strangers to have access to, as this information will travel with the mp3 file wherever it goes. For ALBUM, type the name of the overall class project, like "Radio2008." (Keep this to one easily spelled word to minimize student error.) Select "Spoken Word" for the genre. Click OK to finish.

Uploading to an iPod *or* Burning a CD

1. Add the mp3 file to iTunes. Open iTunes. Go to FILE > IMPORT... to add the file to iTunes. Now build a playlist. A playlist is like a documents folder: it holds virtual copies of your audio recordings; however, a single audio file can be "stored" in multiple playlists. So Jacquie's radio play can be filed in the Radio Plays playlist *and* in the Jacquie2008 playlist for easy retrieval. Go to FILE > NEW PLAYLIST. Now click and drag your mp3 files into the proper playlist. (The mp3 files will also still appear on the main iTunes Library screen.)

2. Burn a CD. Double-click on the playlist you want. Insert a blank CD. Click the Burn CD button in the top-right corner of iTunes.

3. Transfer files to an iPod. Connect the iPod to the computer. When the iPod icon appears in the left column, drag the playlist onto the iPod icon.

Publishing to the Web

Uploading files to the Web requires online storage space. Many school districts have websites that allow teachers to upload any kind of file to a teacher website. If not, discuss other online storage items with the system administrator. One free option is Switchpod (http://www.switchpod.com). Once the audio file is uploaded, place a link to it on a blog or the school's website. Technically, a podcast is like a magazine subscription: subscribers find the podcast series to which they wish to subscribe, and subsquent podcasts added to the series are downloaded automatically by the user's software. This requires setting up an RSS feed such as Feedburner (http://www.feedburner.com). To protect student privacy, be cautious about allowing children to record personal information on a podcast.

These instructions were written for Audacity for Windows XP and iTunes 7.0.2 for Windows. Instructions for other operating systems are similar.

■ RADIO PLAYS

A radio play is a theatrical work that is told through voices. Although standard in the pretelevision days of radio with shows such as *Little Orphan Annie,* during the TV era they became nearly extinct. However, with the advent of podcasting, they are regaining popularity.

Successful student radio plays should have the following elements:

- background research (if telling a moment from history or writing a historical fiction play);
- plenty of dialogue between characters;
- a story told primarily through dialogue, with minimal descriptive paragraphs;
- a narrator who describes the setting at the start of each scene and describes any action that cannot be described through dialogue;
- a written script with clearly marked roles for each participant; and
- sound effects to bring the story to life.

From a dramatic perspective, radio plays allow students to further explore character development, especially the voice. Without the body to rely on for character interpretation, students must focus consciously on sound and the voice for expression.

Step One: Collaborate to Identify a Topic for Study

The model radio play lesson presented here was created to accompany a literature unit on Western Expansion. Because the unit of study was literature, the radio plays will be works of historical fiction, weaving historical facts into a fictional drama. The highest level of Bloom's Taxonomy is Synthesis: the transforming of knowledge into a new creative product. A historical fiction radio play reaches the Synthesis level because research is manipulated, transformed, and integrated into a work of fiction. For educators concerned about plagiarism, radio plays are appealing because they are unique projects that cannot be copied from somewhere else.

Step Two: Develop the Rubric, Project Timeline, and Subtopics

As discussed in prior chapters, folding these decisions into the early planning process ensures that instructors have a mutual vision for the project. It also helps scaffold the process for students and gives students more confidence that the project will be graded fairly and objectively. The sample rubric on page 161 assesses all stages of the project.

**Rubric:
Radio Play**

Name _____

For each section, 1-5 points will be given; 5 points is the highest. The student will self-evaluate. The teacher and media specialist will also evaluate the project and assign the final grade.

RESEARCH

	Self-Evaluation (1-5)	Teacher Evaluation (1-5)
I began my research by reading an encyclopedia entry to gain basic knowledge about our research topic.		
I wrote at least two preliminary research questions to share at our planning conference.		
I participated in planning conferences with my teammates and teacher/media specialist.		
We created a research plan at the first conference.		
My team used at least three online sources for research and printed them out.		
The sources we used were of high quality.		
I highlighted and took notes on my web printouts.		

TEAMING

I worked well as a member of a team.		
Work was equally shared by all teammates.		

PROJECT

Our script is historical fiction.		
Our script contains at least ten accurate facts/historical information.		
Our script has a logical sequence of events.		
Our script has good spelling, punctuation, and capitalization.		
Our script is neatly typed in a script format.		
Our bibliography is complete, neat, and typed.		

PRESENTATION

We began our story by giving the title and our first names (no last names).		
We successfully recorded our play.		
Our play includes original and creative sound effects.		
Our play is enthusiastically presented.		
Voices are interesting and have variety.		

SUBTOTAL:		
TOTAL POINTS (OUT OF 100):		

Brainstorm a list of 10 to 15 possible subtopics for the area of study. For the Western Expansion example, potential subtopics include the Transcontinental Railroad, Buffalo Bill, Daniel Boone, the Alamo, the Gold Rush, the Mormon Trail, the Oregon Trail, Sacagawea, Lewis and Clark, and the Louisiana Purchase.

Step Three: Introduce the Project to Students

Say,

We have been reading several historical fiction and nonfiction narratives about Western Expansion. We've talked about how historical fiction is a fictional, made-up story set in the past that feels realistic because it has details from history in it.

Many of you have enjoyed learning about how the western part of the United States was settled. Now we are going to write our own historical fiction narratives and create radio plays from them. A radio play is a kind of performance in which we can hear, but not see, the action. Characters speak, we hear sound effects, and there might be music, too. Can you think of a time when the television was on at home, but you were in another room? You could hear voices, music, and sounds but had to picture the action in your imagination. That's what a radio play is like. We'll record your radio plays on the computer and publish them online. This is called a *podcast.*

Thinking about the final product—historical fiction radio plays that take place during Western Expansion—let's work backwards. What do you think we will need to know in order to be able to create this play?

(Students provide answers, such as "research," "people to work with," "a topic," "facts," "how to make a radio play" and "how to make a podcast.")

You're right—those are all things we need to know more about before we start. Let's start with people to work with. Your teacher and I randomly divided you into groups of three.

(Call names and ask students to sit with teammates.)

Now, let's work on a topic. On your handout *(distribute instructor-made list of subtopics)* is a list of historical events related to Western Expansion. Your teacher is going to tell you a fact or two about each topic, and then we would like you, as a group, to select a topic that you would enjoy learning more about.

(Students select topics.)

Great—the next thing we need to think about is research. Where do you think we might get some great research sources?

(Students respond with "Google," "encyclopedia," "old books," and "databases," and the instructors discuss each of these options with students.)

As we're researching, we need to keep our overall product in mind–the historical fiction radio play. Keep that in mind as you search through information. The facts you gather should help your story come to life. Remember to keep a printout for each source you use and to use your highlighter to mark important text and to take notes in the margins.

You will use this planning sheet [page 164] to help you stay organized. You can also check your work against this rubric [page 161] to make sure you are on track. You will each receive a project folder. Store all papers in this folder.

You will have two instructor conferences: one to discuss your initial research questions and one to discuss the first draft of your script. Notice the due dates on the bottom of the planning sheet. We will talk more about how to organize your script and how to do the actual recording later in the project.

Now, take a few moments to work with your group. Look over the possible topics, the rubric, and the planning sheet. Decide on a topic that will interest you.

Step Four: Research

The media specialist and classroom teacher work collaboratively during the research process to guide student groups through a meaningful research process. Conferencing, project folders, and note taking are all useful strategies (see chapter 7).

Step Five: Writing the Script

Radio plays require written scripts; they often weaken if improvised. A script is a document containing the words spoken by performers in a play. A radio script also includes sound effects.

A sound effect is a nonspoken sound that helps animate the story. Sound effects can help set atmosphere (thunder and rain) or describe the actions of the play (footsteps, doors slamming). While sound effect CDs can be purchased and imported into Audacity, and advanced software like Garage Band has built-in sound effects libraries, it is a creative challenge for students to create their own sound effects from simple household objects. Making sound effects by hand is rarely practiced today, but Garrison Keillor's radio program *A Prairie Home Companion* still employs a sound effects engineer who makes all sounds without the benefit of technology. For example, to imitate walking, the sound effects engineer might place two shoes on the table in front of the microphone and tap them on the table. Rapping knuckles on a piece of wood simulates a knock on a door. Toothpicks in a hollow tube are reminiscent of rain, while waving a thin aluminum cookie sheet can sound like thunder. Slapping the fingers of one hand against the palm of the other can simulate a cheek being slapped. Musical instruments add melodies and musical motifs.

Scripts are formatted by dividing the page into two columns. In the left column, the name of the character speaking is listed, or the code "SFX" for sound effect is given. In the right column, the character's text or the type of sound effect is given. If the script is being handwritten, consider using the vertical line placed just to the right of the holes on the paper as the dividing line between two columns. On page 165 is an example of a student-created script. Notice how the script begins with a title and that all characters are listed.

Planning Sheet: Radio Play

Name_____

Other Students in Group: _____

_____

Initial Research Questions (What do we need to find out first in our research?)

Roles in Our Play:

Role   Played by

_____

_____

_____

_____

_____

_____

--continue on back side of paper if needed--

We will need these sound effects:

Item   Will be brought/made by:

_____

_____

_____

_____

_____

_____

--continue on back side of paper if needed--

Important Dates:

Project Assigned: _____   Class Rehearsals: _____

Conference #1: _____   Recording Date: _____

In-Class Research Dates: _____   Folder & Rubric Due: _____

Script due: _____

Conference #2: _____

Escaping the Underground Railroad
A radio play by Christian, Jen, Noah, Julia, and Fred

Characters: Narrator, Harriet Tubman, Celeste the slave, Overseer, Master

Narrator:	For over a hundred years before the Civil War, there were slaves in the South. They were not treated as full humans.
SFX:	Whip.
Master:	I'm the master around here, and I'll make the decisions!
Narrator:	Many worked long hours in the fields of plantations.
SFX:	Slaves singing in the fields.
Overseer:	Stop that singing and get back to work!
Narrator:	Sometimes, they were taken away from their families. It was very unfair. Harriet Tubman wanted to help people escape from slavery. She was known as the Moses of her People.
Celeste:	Harriet, take me with you. Take me to the North, where I can be free!
Harriet:	Yes, Celeste. We will leave in the middle of the night and follow the North Star. Listen for my song after midnight.
SFX:	Singing of "Go Down, Moses."
SFX:	Nighttime sounds of crickets.

Groups can collaborate on creating a single radio play script, which can be photocopied by the instructors for rehearsal purposes. Students should keep a copy in their project folders and highlight the part(s) for which they are responsible.

As students solidify their script, the list of characters and sound effects should be recorded on the planning sheet.

Step Six: Conferencing, Rehearsing, and Revising

When students have completed the rough draft of the script and checked it against the rubric guidelines, they may meet with an instructor for a second conference. The purpose of this conference is to check for historical facts embedded in the script, assess the veracity of the facts, and discuss production preparation concerns. For example, if a radio play has ten roles but five actors, discuss how the students will manipulate their voices using pitch, volume, speed, and tone to make each role sound different. Select one student to be the sound effects engineer. The engineer is responsible for setting up his or her sound effects table and running the Audacity software during recording.

Students should then rehearse their script, taking care to warm up their voices using warm-ups from chapter 2. Sound effects should be part of this rehearsal process. Consider giving each group a labeled crate or box in which to store sound effects materials at school. If computers are available, invite students to practice using Audacity to make a sample recording. Students should read their script, leaving pauses for the sound effects. After recording the text, they can follow the podcasting tips sheet (page 159) to add in sound effects later.

During conferencing or rehearsing, a need may arise for more information to flesh out the play. This is a normal, "real world" occurrence; allow opportunities for students to re-research and revise the script as needed.

Step Seven: Recording, Sharing, and Reflection

After a few rehearsals, students are ready to record. Post a copy of the tips sheet (page 159) by each computer. After recording and exporting the files to mp3 format, bring all groups together and share the radio plays. If your media center has a bank of OPAC computers, set them up as listening stations, with one radio play at each station, or play them all through an amplification system so everyone hears them at once.

Radio plays may also be posted online or burned to CD and shared with PTA, parents, Curriculum Night guests, or board of education members. Have a contest for the best CD cover design or host a release party!

After the excitement has ebbed, ask students—either via discussion or via written feedback—to reflect on the success of their project. Here are some questions that might be useful for reflection:

- What did you learn about the research process during this project?
- What did you learn about using your voice during this project?
- How effective was your group at using sound effects to help listeners visualize the setting and actions?
- What are you proud of?
- What would you do differently or better next time?
- How did teamwork help to improve your research and radio play?
- What advice would you give future classes about making a historical fiction radio play?

For formal assessment, collect the project folders and use the rubric on page 161.

■ CONCLUSION

At the time this book was written, podcasts were still an emerging technology. Most focused on sharing informational text in a news broadcast or radio show format. This form of podcasting is motivating, exciting, easy, and inexpensive. When coupled with the power of synthesizing research into a new product for a radio play, it becomes a powerful learning tool.

■ ADDITIONAL RESOURCE

AIMS Multimedia. 1990. *Part 5: Readers Theatre: Historical Fiction.* UnitedStreaming. Available at http://www.unitedstreaming.com (accessed January 15, 2007).

Part III
Puppetry

Chapter 10
Storytelling with Shadow: Shadow Puppetry (Grades K and Up)

■ INTRODUCTION

In a school setting, shadow puppetry is a flexible, graceful, aesthetically pleasing way for students to explore content and demonstrate learning. Shadow puppetry is a dramatic art form in which two-dimensional puppet silhouettes are illuminated from behind and appear on a screen. Items placed between the light source and the screen create shadows.

The opening scene of the Ukrainian folktale "The Mitten," as designed by participants in the 2005 American Professional Partnership for Lithuanian Education seminar. Photography by Gregory L. Strom.

The roots of shadow puppetry are in Indonesia, particularly the island of Java. *Wayang kulit,* the Indonesian expression for shadow puppetry, technically means "shadow screen" but is now considered the general term for shadow puppetry. *Wayang kulit* features a single puppeteer known as the *dalang.* The *dalang* holds the status of priest in traditional Indonesian society. Performing at night, with a screen backlit by oil lamps, the *dalang* retells traditional epic stories, with performances that can last as long as 13 hours! To prepare for performances, the *dalang* designs intricately cut, two-dimensional shadow puppets to represent these epic characters. Usually these puppets are jointed, meaning that the character's arm can move independently of the body, making gesture and characterization easier and more realistic for the viewer. Traditionally the puppets were carefully crafted from leather and intricately painted for the benefit of the wealthy patrons, who sat behind the screen and would be able to appreciate both the painted adornments and the shadows cast by the puppets. (Those of other socioeconomic strata would sit in front of the screen, seeing only the shadow.) Because of their elaborate designs, many historical *wayang kulit* puppets are treasured by art collectors today. Contemporary practitioners of shadow puppetry rarely allow "backstage" audiences, and contemporary puppets are rarely painted today. While the *dalang* creates and operates the puppets, he also supervises and cues a team of accompanying musicians, creating a performance experience unlike any other.

For "The Mitten," icicles made from translucent wax paper and snowflakes made from wax paper and white copy paper hang by sewing thread from bamboo gardening stakes. The stakes are attached to the top of the shadow puppet screen to create scenery that communicate the wintry setting.

Shadow puppets can be constructed out of simple materials, and the shadowy silhouettes create breathtaking performances from student puppeteers. Students are fascinated by the powers of light and shadow and are engaged with the art form. Because shadow puppetry is a visual medium, it is particularly attractive to students who struggle to represent themselves via text.

Shadow puppetry can showcase the skills of artistically gifted students, who can craft intricately cut puppets. At the same time, it is successful with less artistic students. Because only the shadow is seen—never the puppet itself—during performance, students can literally cut-and-paste until they create a puppet that pleases them. Simply put, shadow puppetry is as easy as a craft but with the impact of fine art.

A shadow puppet performance is a synthesis of student understanding, narrative text, and visual representation. When students engage in the full puppetry process, drafting their own scripts, adapting existing text or researching a historical topic, creating puppets, and ultimately synthesizing what is learned into a unique shadow puppet performance, they reach the highest level of thinking on Bloom's Taxonomy. Like many of the projects described in this book, shadow puppet projects are equally effective as learning activities or as an assessment of student learning. Performance-based work provides opportunity for students to develop personal and workforce skills like teamwork, sharing, taking turns, negotiating, reaching compromise, brainstorming, and more. And the excitement of shadow puppetry provides a way of learning that taps into students' intrinsic motivation.

As can many of the other techniques in this book, shadow puppetry can be used to enhance understanding of literature or as a means of demonstrating what has been learned through research.

■ STEP ONE: COLLABORATE TO SELECT A STORY TO ENACT

In addition to partnering with a classroom teacher, consider collaborating with a music teacher, who could work with students to create an overture, musical motifs, and sound effects, and/or an art teacher who can work with students to create effective silhouettes for puppets, intriguing puppet details, and overall artistry and craftsmanship.

Examine the curriculum to find areas where more student engagement would be beneficial. Scripts can be selected from a reader's theatre book or Web site, but adapting an existing story allows for more creative flexibility, choral work, and a script that is custom-fit to the shadow puppetry medium. When choosing a story to adapt into a script, consider the same sorts of stories that were effective with narrative pantomime or circle drama (see chapter 3), using the following questions:

- Is there a lot of action in the story? Action makes for stronger puppetry. Too much "standing around and talking" is not interesting for the puppeteer or viewer.

- Are there enough roles for the entire class? Or are there just a few roles so that a small group can handle the play?

- Can an interesting narrative, with rich language, be created?

- Does it connect to the curriculum in a meaningful way?

- Is the play of a manageable length? For elementary students a play lasting five to ten minutes is adequate. Plays longer than this often have far more complicated scenery requirements and more characters, and demand a longer rehearsal schedule than many busy curriculum plans can accommodate.

- Can the scenery be managed by just a few students? This will affect how many kids can be involved, the complexity of scene changes, and the amount of time that may have to be invested in scenery.

- Is copyright permission required, or does the project fall within fair use guidelines? All work, once it is written down in print or online, is automatically copyrighted, even if it doesn't say "Copyright 2005" on it. If choosing a published story, be sure the project is within the "fair use" guidelines of the U.S. laws on copyright. Fair use is the section of copyright law that allows educators to use copyrighted material in their classrooms without penalty. Generally, as long as a puppet play stays within the classroom, it falls within fair use guidelines, but fair use may not apply if the play will be recorded, broadcast, or performed before a nonclassroom audience. Consult Stanford University's fair use site (http://fairuse.stanford.edu/Copyright_and_Fair_Use_Overview/chapter9/index.html) for guidance.

- Will there be a partnership with another teacher, such as an art or music teacher? Are there rich visual images and the possibility of adding musical overtures and motifs?

- Does the action depend on small, detailed props? For example, the story of William Tell requires that an arrow strike the apple on his son's head, and the Cinderella story needs slippers. These tiny details can be hard to re-create realistically in a puppet performance.

■ STEP TWO: WRITE AND FORMAT THE SCRIPT

After a story has been selected, it can be made into a script. Scripts are discussed in chapter 9, and a similar format can be used here.

One shadow puppetry strategy is to use narrators instead of asking puppeteers to speak in the voice of their puppets. Using narrators lets puppeteers focus solely on the backstage choreography and the onscreen staging. Narrators can stand to the side of the screen and be more easily heard than puppeteers speaking from behind the screen. With early elementary students, a single narrator—either the instructor or a student—is easiest. For upper elementary or older students, two narrators allows more complex textual delivery such as choral readings.

Strategies for Adapting a Text

When adapting a text into a script, streamline the narrative. Remove extended passages of description. Focus on action and dialogue instead. Use the choral reading strategies discussed in chapter 8 to emphasize particular pieces of text. This layering produces a more complex, textured sound that adds dimensionality and interest to the play.

If partnering with a music specialist, consider moments when puppet characters' reactions, personalities, and behaviors can be emphasized through music. For example, if the play is *The Three Little Pigs,* a drum beat could be used when the wolf knocks on the door. The ominous drum sound heightens the drama.

Sample Adaptation

This example uses a public domain text. (All works published prior to 1926 are in the public domain and can be used or adapted without violating U.S. copyright laws.) Sacred-Texts.com has digitally reproduced Dr. James A. Honey's' 1910 book of South African folktales. "Cloud Eating" comes from that Web site and is available at http://www.sacred-texts.com/afr/saft/sft27.htm . This brief creation myth or *pourquoi* tale was originally printed like this:

Cloud Eatin
A South African Folktale
Recorded by James A. Honey, M.D.

JACKAL and Hyena were together, it is said, when a white cloud rose. Jackal descended upon it, and ate of the cloud as if it were fat. When he wanted to come down, he said to Hyena, "My sister, as I am going to divide with thee, catch me well." So she caught him, and broke his fall. Then she also went up and ate there, high up on the top of the cloud. When she was satisfied, she said, "My grayish brother, now catch me well." The grayish rogue said to his friend, "My sister, I shall catch thee well. Come therefore down." He held up his hands, and she came down from the cloud, and when she was near, Jackal cried out (painfully jumping to one side), "My sister, do not take it ill. Oh me! Oh me! A thorn has pricked me and sticks in me." Thus she fell down from above, and was sadly hurt. Since that day, it is said that Hyena's hind feet have been shorter and smaller than the front ones.

Source: http://www.sacred-texts.com/afr/saft/sft27.htm

This text has a simple plot. The animal characters will require student research in order to make accurate puppets, and the presence of the cloud will be a challenge. The story can be told in a single scene, without scenery, making it a simple story for a class's first introduction to shadow puppetry. However, it has some outdated language.

Page 175 shows how Honey's text could be divided into a script for two narrators. A few strategies have been employed here. Notice how the two narrators alternate telling the story, but Narrator 1 consistently says Jackal's lines and Narrator 2 consistently says Hyena's lines. This preserves character consistency. Narrators can be encouraged to develop these vocal characters by varying their voice pitch, speed, tone, and volume (see chapter 2 for warm-up exercises students can do to extend their vocal range).

Sometimes the narrative is spoken jointly in a choral reading style. This creates a more interesting texture and adds extra "punch" to exciting, meaningful, or especially important text.

The quality of writing has been changed a bit to reflect twenty-first-century speaking patterns and to make the performance of the words easier for student narrators.

Finally, notice how some limited stage directions are included in the script. Stage directions, written in italics and enclosed by parentheses, give the puppeteers some initial guidance about how the characters should move and behave. More details can be filled in during the rehearsal process. Adapting a script like this can take approximately 30 minutes.

■ STEP THREE: DECIDE ON AN ASSESSMENT STRATEGY

As with other projects in this book, shadow puppet projects can be unassessed explorations or evaluated activities. If evaluated, choose an assessment that fits your learners, their age, and their curriculum goals. The following criteria may help in designing an assessment.

Research Skills (if required by the project)

- Does the student participate in planning conferences or production meetings?
- Does the student engage in a meaningful research process?
- Does the student select appropriate print or online resources?
- Does the student document the research process with note cards, highlighted printouts, or a bibliography?
- Is there evidence of accurate research in the script (if applicable)?

Writing Skills (if required by the project)

- If a script is created by students, are a beginning, middle and end present?
- Is there rich, descriptive language?
- Does the script follow appropriate writing conventions?

Cloud-Eating
A South African Folktale recorded by James A. Honey, MD, and adapted by Kristin Fontichiaro

1:      One day, Jackal and Hyena were together. Suddenly,

1&2:   a white cloud rose!

(The cloud rises.)

2:      Jackal, being a greedy animal, leapt onto it, eating the cloud like cotton candy.

(Jackal jumps up, sits on cloud, eats. Hyena watches.)

1:      After his belly was full, he wanted to come down. He called down to Hyena. *(Leans over edge of cloud.)* "My sister! I have eaten all the cloud my belly will hold. Catch me when I jump down, and then it can be your turn."

2:      Hyena agreed. *(Hyena nods.)* She caught Jackal when he leapt down.

(Jackal leaps down, lands on Hyena.)

1:      Then she jumped up onto the cloud and ate until her belly was full.

(Hyena jumps up, sits on cloud, eats. Jackal watches.)

2:      *(Hyena leans over cloud.)* "My brother!" called Hyena. "I have eaten all the cloud my belly will hold. Catch me when I jump down."

1:      Jackal held up his paws *(holds up paws)*

1 & 2: and Hyena jumped! *(She jumps.)*

1:      When she was near the ground, Jackal cried out! (He jumps in pain.) Now you know that Jackal is a famous trickster. "My sister!" he said. "Oh, oh, oh! I've been pricked by a thorn!"

2:      Poor Hyena. She

1&2:   fell *(Hyena falls)*

2:      to the ground and was

1&2:   badly hurt.

1:      And from that day on, Hyena's hind feet have always been shorter and smaller than the front ones.

Aesthetic Skills

- Does the puppet accurately reflect the character's personality or, in the case of a researched person or animal, its characteristics?
- If operating a puppet, does the puppet move well across the stage?
- If operating scenery, does the scenery operator make smooth blackout and scenery changes?
- Does the scenery help portray the setting effectively?
- If the student is the narrator, is it easy to understand him or her?
- Is the narrator's volume loud enough?
- Does the narrator speak slowly and clearly enough that the words can be heard easily?

Work Skills

- Does the student make a genuine effort?
- Does the student work well as part of a group?
- Does the student appear prepared?
- Does the student participate in planning conferences or production meetings?
- Does the student keep research or scripts in a project folder?

■ STEP FOUR: SET UP THE PUPPET STAGE

Many children grow up learning how to make some light shadows. By arranging their hands in a particular shape and holding them between the light cast by a bare household lamp and the wall, shadows are created on the wall. With shadow puppetry, the light is focused not on the wall but on a screen that separates the audience from the backstage puppeteers. A puppet is held between the light source and the screen, thus creating the shadow. If the puppet is held very close to the screen, the projected image will be the same size as the puppet. The closer to the light source a puppet is held, the larger it becomes.

As shown in the diagram on page 177, the screen separates the audience from the performers. The performers and their puppets are behind the screen, or backstage.

Shadow puppet screens can be made from a variety of materials: wooden frames, rolling bulletin boards with a hole cut in the center, even a sheet draped in the doorway.

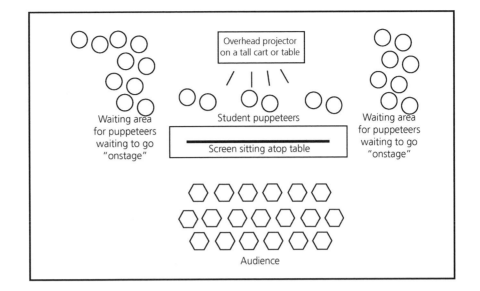

For portable, inexpensive tabletop screens, try making a screen from ¾-inch PVC pipe, the white plastic pipe used by plumbers. It is lightweight and inexpensive, and can be assembled quickly. Segments of straight PVC pipe are attached with PVC connectors, making them easy to assemble and disassemble. PVC pipes come in lengths of eight feet or more. Some home improvement centers will cut PVC to size for free. If this service is not available, buy a ratcheting PVC cutter to make the job easier; these cost $12–15 at a home improvement store and require little hand strength. A saw will also work but is less portable, more time-consuming, and less safe in classroom settings. The total cost for enough PVC pipe to make a four-by-two-foot screen should be less than $10.

Shadow puppet screens can be any width or height. For small group projects, a square screen two feet tall and two feet long works well, as it parallels the shape of the light projected from behind by an overhead projector. However, if doing a project with an entire class, a long rectangular screen that is four feet long and two feet tall provides more playing space and backstage maneuvering room.

The diagram on page 178 shows how to make a rectangular or square screen from PVC pipe. For the screen's fabric, a white plastic shower curtain liner is an inexpensive, easily obtainable material. Other options are white stretch-knit fabric, a white bedsheet, or a white plastic banquet tablecloth (available in large roles at party supply stores). Attach plastic materials to the frame with book tape or clear plastic mailing tape, pulling the material taut (but not so taut that the frame begins to buckle). Attach fabric with book tape or duct tape. The following photos show what a completed frame would look like.

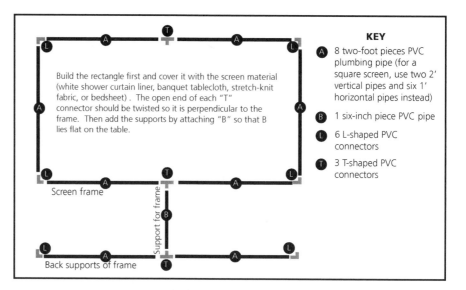

Build the rectangle first and cover it with the screen material (white shower curtain liner, banquet tablecloth, stretch-knit fabric, or bedsheet). The open end of each "T" connector should be twisted so it is perpendicular to the frame. Then add the supports by attaching "B" so that B lies flat on the table.

Screen frame

Support for frame

Back supports of frame

KEY

Ⓐ 8 two-foot pieces PVC plumbing pipe (for a square screen, use two 2' vertical pipes and six 1' horizontal pipes instead)

Ⓑ 1 six-inch piece PVC pipe

Ⓛ 6 L-shaped PVC connectors

Ⓣ 3 T-shaped PVC connectors

A 4-by-2-foot rectangular screen made of PVC pipe as seen from the audience. Notice how the projector is placed far in the background to allow plenty of space for students to move between the screen and the projector.

The same screen as seen from the puppeteers' backstage perspective.

When the screen is assembled, place it on top of a table. (For large screens, push two tables together.) Behind the screen, place an overhead projector on a tall A/V cart. If the school lacks an overhead projector, light your shadow play with an inexpensive, simple construction clip lamp (the kind with an aluminum reflecting "bowl" surrounding a bare light bulb). These are available for a few dollars at home improvement stores, though they lack some of the creative flexibility of overhead projectors.

An overhead projector not only provides a large and high-powered light, but it offers tremendous flexibility for creative puppetry. With an overhead projector, students can create puppetry effects in three ways:

1. by holding puppets against the screen makes a shadow that is the same size as the puppet;
2. by laying puppets down on the overhead projector's glass surface to create huge, looming shadows; and
3. by moving puppets forward and backward between the projection lamp and the screen to make objects look like they are flying.

Overhead projectors also cast a more powerful light than many other light sources, making crisper, more defined shadows.

In this image, taken from a student experimentation session, a puppet of a horse was laid down on the glass, making it appear much larger than the sun, man, and butterfly puppets, which were held against the screen and are not magnified.

The overhead projector makes scenery easy, too. Scenery can be drawn with a permanent marker on a blank transparency. Place the transparency on the glass for an instant backdrop. For this to work, the distance between the screen and the projector must remain constant during each rehearsal. Make small marks on the floor with electrical tape or the hook side of a piece of Velcro™ to help mark the spot. A simple and dramatic effect can be achieved using colored theatrical gel —made of a heat-resistant plastic that professional theatre companies place in their overhead lights—to create a moody background rich with atmospheric color.

Allow at least five feet between the projector and the table so that students have ample room to move around the equipment and each other, as shown on page 177. If the table or overhead cart has wheels, lock them in place. Try to position the overhead projector near a wall plug so that children working behind the screen won't trip over the cord. Lay carpet tape over the cord as a safety precaution. If a nearby plug is not available and the cord must travel a distance, cut spare carpet into strips and tape it over the cord.

Turn on the overhead projector and turn off the room lights. Adjust the distance between the projector and the screen so that the projector's light extends a bit beyond the projector's screen. Lighting professionals call this extension of light *spill light,* because it "spills" beyond its designated area. To keep spill light out of the audience's eyes, tape white duplicating paper along the edges of the projector, slowly moving the paper until the projector's light reaches just to the edge of the screen. This is called masking. Avoid taping directly onto the glass. Instead, tape to the metal or plastic frame around the edges of the glass. Adjust the masking before each session.

▪ STEP FIVE: INTRODUCE THE PROJECT WITH A DEMONSTRATION

Begin by saying,

> In social studies, we have been studying the nations of Africa, and in language arts, we have been reading folktales from many African nations. Today we will begin creating shadow plays based on traditional stories from South Africa. Each group will receive a *pourquoi* tale that they will turn into a shadow play. *Pourquoi* is a French word meaning, "why," and *pourquoi* tales were told in ancient times to explain why things are the way they are. Each group will receive a different play to create.
>
> A shadow play is a kind of story in which the characters appear as shadows. These shadows are created using this screen, these paper puppets, and this overhead projector behind the screen.

In *Worlds of Shadow* (1997), authors and puppeteers Donna Wisniewski and David Wisniewski outline the importance of demonstrating the effects of light and shadow to students. A demonstration can take as little as 15 minutes and is time well spent. It builds excitement and enthusiasm for the project and helps students envision the new art form. Based on the Wisniewskis' recommendations, I explore the following concepts in my demos for students:

1. **How shadows are made with rear-projected light sources.** A shadow occurs when something gets between the light and the screen. Put a hand behind the screen as an example. Your hand blocks the light from getting to the screen, making a shadow.

2. **Opacity.** An item that is *opaque* does not let light shine through it. Ask students to look around the room. What can students find that is opaque? Wood? Books? Desks? What happens when an opaque item is held behind the screen? Demonstrate by holding familiar classroom items—a book, a pencil, a pair of scissors, a hand and arm—behind the screen.

3. **Silhouettes.** A *silhouette* is the outline shape of a shadow. Invite a student to stand behind the screen, facing the side. This "side view" is known as profile. Notice how the silhouette shows a few loose hairs, the nose, and the shape of the chin, even a few wisps of hair. The silhouette of a shadow puppet is very important for communicating information about the puppet's character to the audience. Point out to students that silhouettes in shadow puppetry communicate much more than a front-facing view.

4. **Transparency.** An item that is *transparent* is see-through. What items in the classroom are transparent? A window? An overhead transparency? A Lucite™ box on the teacher's desk? Clear cellophane tape? (Be careful here: shiny clear plastic tape is transparent; frosted or Scotch™ Magic tape is translucent.) Demonstrate by holding these items behind the screen.

5. **Translucency.** Things that aren't quite opaque and aren't quite transparent are *translucent*. An item that is translucent lets some light pass through. What items do students see in the room that are translucent? A colored plastic ruler? A jewel? A piece of stained glass? The plastic cap from a can of potato chips?

6. **Items that are part opaque and part transparent**. What if eyeglasses are placed behind the screen? What will happen? (Result: the frames are opaque and make a shadow, but the lenses—unless they are really dirty or are sunglasses—will be transparent.)

7. **Making puppets.** Say, "When we create a shadow play, we use the ideas of opaque, transparent, and translucent materials to help us make puppets, scenery, and backdrops for our play. The materials we choose help tell the story to our audience."

8. **Demonstrate with sample puppets.** Talk about the opaque, transparent, and translucent parts.

9. **Show a few colored theatrical gels.** When creating stage productions, lighting designers place heat-resistant colored plastic in front of lights. This plastic is known as *gel.* When gel is placed on the glass of an overhead projector, the entire screen turns that color. These colors can help establish mood or setting. For example, a red gel might make the audience think of fire, whereas a blue gel might denote evening. Green gel could create a grassy slope, and brown gel creates a mountain. Place some sample colors on the overhead projector. What does color do to set a mood? What happens when colors overlap? For example, a blue gel layered with a yellow gel will make green.

10. **Experiment with waxed paper.** The Wisniewskis include waxed paper in their demonstration. As they point out, it makes quick and inexpensive scenery. Place it on an angle on the glass, and it can be a hill. Place it horizontally, and it reveals a snowy ground. Crinkle it up for a spider web. Cut or tear it into triangles to make a mountain range.

■ STEP SIX: GIVE STUDENTS TIME TO PLAY AND EXPERIMENT

Students are naturally drawn to light and shadow. Following a demonstration, students need time to experiment with shadow puppetry prior to beginning a formal project. Schedule small groups of up to ten students to visit the puppetry area. Give them time to make "rabbit ears" and "barking dogs" with their hands. Let them experiment with some sample puppets and theatrical gels. This is the ideal time for them to test out color theory and the concepts of transparency, translucency, and opacity.

This uninterrupted exploration time is important for building students' interest and motivation in the project. Consider making the puppetry area a learning center for a day or so. First graders can sustain up to 20 minutes of unstructured play. Older students may not need this dedicated time, but it remains important to have a screen and overhead projector set up throughout the process so they can test out their puppets and refine them.

STEP SEVEN: MAKE PUPPETS

**Shadow puppets can be simple one-piece puppets. This puppet is made
from heavy watercolor paper with a shish kebob skewer taped with
mailing tape at the bottom.**

Puppets in shadow plays are created to represent characters and scenery. One
useful strategy for making puppets is to consider them as functional objects that
are meant to be seen as shadows, not as works of art that can be used both in a play
and as displays for an art show. Students with weaker visual or artistic skills need
the flexibility of being able to paste pieces onto their puppet or to sketch an idea on
the back that is later discarded. Liberate students from the expectation that the
puppets must be "beautiful" when seen up close. This lessens student anxiety and
makes puppet making more accessible and flexible for your students.

Making Puppets with Students

In most cases, educators work with an entire classroom of children, with either the entire class working on a single play or several small groups each creating
its own play.

One good starting point is to convene a production meeting. Production
meetings are commonplace in professional theatrical companies. In professional
companies, production meetings are held regularly with key players in attendance.

The producer, director, costume designer, scenic designer, lighting designer, props master or mistress, stage manager, and others responsible for designing or bringing to life the look and feel of a stage production meet to organize the work schedule, share ideas, update each other on progress, and make sure that the production is coming together cohesively. During a production meeting, instructors can introduce the project, assign roles, and brainstorm a list of needed characters, scenery, effects, and props.

One of the first decisions to make is, "Who will make which puppet?" Try to keep this part flexible by posing the question in this way, instead of, "Who wants to be Cinderella?" This is important because later in the process, staging needs may require other students to manipulate the puppet.

Once this is decided, the second question is, "What should we use to make the puppet bodies?" Puppet bodies can also be made from a manila folder, heavy watercolor paper, two layers of paper grocery bags glued together in advance with watery white glue, or cardstock. Thinner paper like construction paper is too floppy, and heavy corrugated cardboard is too difficult for students to cut. Poster board can be used for large, simple shapes but is difficult to manipulate for detailed work.

Another production meeting question is, "How big should the puppets be?" Scale is so important when working with puppets. Puppets should be in relative proportion to one another. For many student projects, asking students to make puppets that fill the entire page of an 8½-by-11-inch piece of cardstock is enough to achieve this goal. However, with other projects, more guidance may be required.

For example, a class is creating a shadow play retelling the story of Jan Brett's *The Mitten*. This text is wonderful for a whole class activity because it has many roles. It includes human characters, a large mitten, and animals of varying sizes. Puppets for this project will be made of 22-by-14-inch pieces of poster board (a standard-sized poster board cut in half). In order to gain proportion, work with the class to set size guidelines. For example, the humans and the mitten will take an entire piece. Large animals such as the bear would fill half a piece. Smaller animals like the rabbit would fill one-quarter of a piece, and the tiny mouse would take just one-eighth of a piece of paper. By regulating how much paper each puppeteer receives up front, much can be done to regulate size and scale.

An option is for students to sketch out their puppets on scratch paper prior to drawing them out on the "real paper." This is not required, and it may be more efficient for students to sketch on the actual medium, as their pencil marks will not be seen by the audience during the final performance. Some simple steps can make sketching a puppet easier for students:

- **Partner with the art specialist**, who may be able to incorporate this project into his or her curriculum.

- **Break down a character into its basic shapes.** For example, a cat is basically a round head, an oval body, four rectangular legs, triangles for ears, and a small rectangular neck. Draw the basic shapes, then smooth the rough shapes with pencil.

- For students in grades three and above, consider **drawing figures in profile** instead of frontal positions. This allows your puppet to "look" at other puppets, which aids in humanizing them for the audience. Making puppets in profile may be too difficult for lower elementary students.

- If puppets are drawn out of scale, consider taking the student's sketch to a duplicating machine and using the **machine's enlarging and reducing** features until it is in scale with the others. The student can then cut it out and trace it onto the puppet medium, or you can print it directly onto cardstock.

- **Use clip art.** Microsoft users may access the Microsoft Template Gallery (http://office. microsoft.com/en-us/templates/default.aspx), which has thousands of clip art templates. In the "Search" box at the top, select "Clip Art and Media," and type in a search term such as "giraffe". Once the first set of search results is shown, you can narrow your search by clicking the "Search" box again and selecting "Clip Art." Follow the instructions for download, then insert it into Microsoft Word™ by going to INSERT > CLIP ART and selecting that image. Click on one of the image's "corners" to expand it to fill an entire page, print it on cardstock, and cut out details, for an instant puppet.

Cutting Out a Puppet (Lower Elementary)

In general, the basic shape of the puppet can be cut out easily with a pair of standard scissors. Add dimension by using inexpensive decorative-edged scissors such as those used for scrapbooking. These scissors, available at craft stores, come in many different patterns. Use them to make a ruffle for the bottom of a dress, "feathers" for an owl, "fur" on a bear's back, and more. They are an inexpensive way to elevate the students' puppets' appearance.

If the puppet requires thin, intricate shapes, consider adding items like wire or pipe cleaners instead of cutting them from the puppet medium. For example, it is much easier for a six-year-old to tape a pair of wire antennae to a ladybug puppet than it is to cut out the antennae.

Hands and faces can be difficult cutting areas for young elementary students. Consider making "mittens" instead of five-fingered hands. For some students, making a blank face and taping on the profile of a nose later may be easier than cutting around the nose on the face.

For really fast puppet making, try an Ellison die-cut shape.

Cutting Out a Puppet (Upper Elementary)

For puppeteers in grades 4 and up, more intricate beauty can be achieved by adding cut details with a razor blade or art knife (X-Acto™ is the most common brand). Inexpensive plastic utility knives may be purchased in multipacks at dollar stores or hardware stores. Some school districts have policies about knives and razor blades in school. Consult district policy prior to using these items with students. The art specialist may be aware of specific policies on using these items in the context of an art project. Using small, single blades allows elaborate shapes to be cut either around the exterior perimeter of the puppet or to cut shapes *inside* the puppet, as shown on page 187.

Demonstrate safe knife operation to students. Students should always cut away from their bodies, not drag the knife toward their torsos. The fingers steadying the puppet material on the table should be kept far from the knife. Carefully inventory the number of knives at the beginning and end of each class.

Place a folded-up section of the newspaper, a cutting board, or a magazine under the puppet so that knife cuts will not damage the table.

Fixing Mistakes

Puppet revisions are easy with shadow puppetry. Because puppetry is two-dimensional, and because the audience will never see the actual puppet, only its shadow, cut-and-paste makes changes easy. Rarely does a puppet need to be remade from scratch. Simply cut off the problematic part of the puppet and tape on a new part.

Clear, shiny tape is a useful tool with shadow puppets. Unlike glue, it doesn't require drying time, so that a student can immediately start working after making a repair. Clear, shiny plastic tape is almost completely transparent, so if it sticks out a little bit past the puppet, it won't be noticed. Avoid the more expensive frosted cellophane tape, as it creates a translucent haze when a transparency is preferred. Book tape or clear plastic mailing tape works for larger areas and strengthens delicate parts.

Accessorizing the Puppet

While puppets are beautiful as simple dark shadows against the light screen, detailed accessories add panache and beauty. *Accessories* are items that add color, texture, or detailing to a puppet. Lace, scraps of theatrical lighting gel, waxed paper, pipe cleaners, string, yarn, tissue paper, or pieces of transparency film decorated with Sharpie™ markers are all examples of accessories.

- Cut out a shape inside the puppet and fill it with colored theatrical gel. For example, you can cut out holes for Goldilocks's eyes and layer blue gel to give her blue eyes.
- Add a real piece of lace to the bottom of a puppet's skirt.
- Add translucent wings to an insect puppet by making them out of waxed paper or colored plastic wrap. (Add even more dimension by crinkling up the waxed paper before cutting it out.)
- Add a braid of yarn to Rapunzel's head to mimic her long hair.
- Add patterns to Prince Charming's robes with a hole punch. Cover the empty spaces with gel for a colorful effect. Cut holes in his crown and fill them with jewel-colored gel for a regal touch.
- Need more details? Consider drawing on a piece of clear transparency film. Then cut out the drawing and tape it to the puppet. (We did this once when a girl struggled to add a pirate flag to her pirate ship puppet. Cutting out a square piece of film and drawing a skull and bones on it was much easier than cutting a pirate logo!)
- Need fine lines? Use pipe cleaners.
- A row of paper clips adds life to the back of a porcupine or stegosaurus puppet.
- Invite students to bring items from home. See what else they can come up with!

Puppet Joints

This puppet has one joint at the shoulder. One support controls the puppet body; the other control moves the arm.

So far the focus has been on puppets made from a single piece. One-piece puppets are appropriate for students up to third grade or for puppets with little or no movement, such as chairs or trees. Students in higher grades are ready for puppets that can move. Puppets with moving parts are created by adding joints. *Joints* are places on a human or animal body where two body parts connect. Each part can move independently of one another. Human joints are found at the shoulder, elbow, wrist, waist, knees, and ankles. When the ankle is the joint, the foot is able to articulate, or move, in a different direction from the leg.

Jointed puppets allow characters to *move* onstage. Moving a leg can indicate walking. A moving arm can reach, shake, embrace, push, or pull.

Making joints requires advance planning. For examples, students wishing to make a puppet with a movable arm cannot simply sketch out a puppet, cut off the arm, and then reattach it. The arm will be too short, creating unnatural proportions. Instead, students should sketch out the body of the puppet, rounding off the shoulder and torso. They should then sketch out the *entire* arm and cut out both parts. Make sure each piece has enough overlap so that when the puppet moves, the joint appears natural. If additional interior detailing is desired, cut out interior designs with the craft knife prior to assembling the puppet.

Next, align the arm with the body. Use a small awl, sharp pencil, or end of a pair of sharp scissors to help students punch a small hole where the brad will go. Young students may need an adult's assistance poking through two layers. A hole punch is not recommended, as it punches holes that are larger than the head of the brad, allowing light to shine through the edges. Place a brad through the two holes. Trim the ends of the brad if they extend beyond the puppet.

Adding Supports

Once the puppet is completed, it is ready to be mounted onto its support. A *support* is the stick onto which the puppet is placed. Supports should be long enough that the puppet can be held up against the screen without the puppeteer's hand or arm becoming visible. Rigid supports create puppets that won't wobble. Slim supports do not distract the viewer from the puppet. Use adjustable pliers or wire nippers to cut the bottom of a dry cleaning hanger for a long, sturdy support. Other options are thin wooden dowels, shish kebab skewers, bamboo gardening stakes, or rigid straws.

If using a jointed puppet as described above, mount the body of the puppet onto one stick, to be held with one hand. The puppet arm will have a second stick that will be held in the other hand. Use clear plastic mailing tape to secure puppets to their supports. Although this may appear an unorthodox art supply, it has several benefits. If some tape appears off the edge of the puppet, it's transparent and will not be seen. Mailing tape also allows supports to detach easily from the puppet. Just score the tape gently along the edge of the stick with your scissors to slip out the stick. This technique is useful for storing puppets from year to year.

How Many Parts Should a Puppet Have?

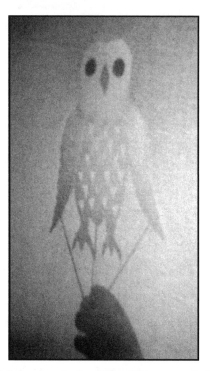

This puppet has joints at each shoulder. The supports for each wing are attached so they can be operated with one hand while the other hand holds the support for the body.

The Wisniewskis, in *Worlds of Shadow,* remind us that a puppet should never have more joints than the puppeteer has hands: two! However, during a professional development seminar I led for Lithuanian teachers, they found creative ways to overrule the rule of two.

One teacher made an owl puppet with joints for the two wings (page 188). How was she going to operate the bird's body AND two wings? I asked. That would take three hands. She flipped her puppet over to the back, where she had fashioned a Y-shaped harness. Each of the top parts of the "Y" connected to one of the wings, and she held the "bottom" of the Y with her hand. As she pulled it up and down, both wings flapped simultaneously.

Another teacher made a bear, with all four legs attached by brads. How was that going to work? I wondered. Then she showed me. She had attached a single stick to the base of her bear. But, she showed me, when she swung the stick gently as she moved the bear forward, the four legs swung, creating an effect she liked very much.

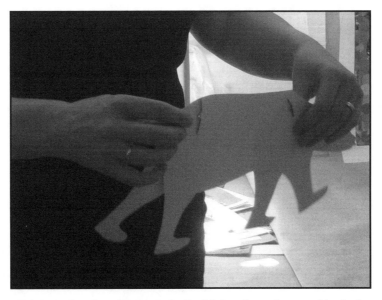

This bear has four legs attached with brads to the top of its body and only a single support.

As a rule of thumb for students, two parts—or two supports—are probably adequate.

Storing Puppets

Because most shadow puppet projects will be focused on performance, it may take several days of rehearsals to prepare. Between rehearsals, storage for the puppets is needed.

Puppets can be stored upright or flat. They can be stored upright in large jars or pots filled with marbles. Another idea is to purchase stiff Styrofoam (not floral foam) and poke the puppet supports into it. Label each hole with the name of the puppet for quick and easy inventory. Give one student the role of "props master" and ask him or her to take inventory before the end of each class. To store puppets flat, try an under-the-bed storage box. Use brown mailing paper or bulletin board paper to separate layers. If you're doing multiple productions at once, consider a separate box for each production. Turn a pair of milk crates upside-down and stick the puppet supports into the open spaces of the crate. (One crate can be placed on either side of the stage and used to hold puppets during performances as well.) In addition, puppets can be stored on horizontal racks designed to hold wet paintings.

■ STEP EIGHT: CREATE SCENERY

Scenery elements are the backgrounds and inanimate objects placed on a stage to help the audience know where a play is taking place. Scenery can be made with puppets, colored gel, waxed paper, found objects and fabric, or images drawn onto transparency film. Assign one or two students to operate the projector and manipulate the scenery.

Scenery with Puppets

Scenery can be made easily with puppets. Setting can be established with puppets made in the shape of trees, fences, snowflakes, buildings, chairs, or columns. Holding these puppets still so that the setting appears realistic can be difficult for young performers. Place a chair with the back facing the screen behind the stage so students can balance their arms, or tape the puppet to the edge of the frame or table to hold it steady.

Scenery with Colored Theatrical Gels

As mentioned in the demonstration, colored gels used for theatrical lighting can be manipulated in various ways to help express the mood of a play or its setting. Students can place gel on the overhead glass to bathe the entire screen in a color. For example, a deep blue gel might indicate evening, while a turquoise gel might indicate an underwater scene. Another choice is to place one colored gel on the top of the glass and a second color on the bottom of the glass. For example, turquoise on top and green on bottom might indicate sky and a grassy field. Using gel to cover part of the screen, leaving the remainder blank, can create abstract scenery. A square piece of yellow gel placed on the glass can represent a house or building. Placing a green gel at an angle indicates a hill. A thin stripe of red at the bottom of the screen can symbolize desert sand.

A sheet of gel costs approximately $7 and is available from theatrical supply companies. Check with the high school drama department or local theatrical companies for advice about suppliers. The two leading gel manufacturers are Lee and Rosco. Six colors will be adequate for most projects: Red (Lee 024), Fuchsia (Roscolux 44), Green (Lee 124), Turquoise (Lee 115), Yellow (Lee 101), and Evening Blue (Lee 75).

Waxed Paper

As shown in the demonstration, waxed paper is a less expensive but equally expressive choice for scenery. As outlined in *Worlds of Shadow,* experiment with ripped or cut pieces of waxed paper to create mountains, tunnels, buildings, curtains, leaves, or snow.

Found Objects and Fabrics

Invite your students to help find objects and fabrics that make interesting scenery patterns. For example, the Wisniewskis placed lace on the glass for fairy tales. Bubble wrap makes an interesting outer space effect. Tulle or netting, available by the yard at fabric stores, creates tiny patterns. Plants, grasses, and Queen Anne's lace also make for intriguing screen patterns.

Images Drawn on Transparency Film

Images can also be drawn on overhead transparencies using colored permanent markers. Avoid wipe-off transparency markers like Vis-a-Vis™ because they may smudge during rehearsals. This method requires patience and skill; the overhead projector and screen must be placed and focused in exactly the same way for each rehearsal and performance.

Scene Changes

With young students, the easiest way to transition between scene changes may be to place a folder over the projector light to "black out" the scenery. Students then turn off the projector, change the scenery, turn on the projector, and wait for a cue from the puppeteers to lift the folder to reveal the new scene. Rehearsing nonverbal cues like this helps the performance run more smoothly and professionally.

■ STEP NINE: REHEARSE

As do the other activities in this book, shadow puppetry focuses not only on content but on strengthening arts techniques. Consider the following areas when planning a rehearsal:

- **Create a group-wide cue for when you will be starting.** One effective way to do this is to play a few moments of introductory music to prepare the audience and cue the performers to begin. The ringing of a triangle, the addition of a live overture, or playing prerecorded music gives everyone a few seconds to get organized.

- **Encourage hand signals** instead of backstage conversation. As a company, create gestures to represent:

    "It's your turn now!"
    "Let's trade places."
    "Please move out of my way."
    "We're ready for the next scene."
    "Please hand that to me."

- **Treat the puppet screen like a stage.** Characters can enter from stage left (the puppeteer's left) or stage right (the puppeteer's right). However, unless they are emerging from underground, characters should not "pop up" from the bottom of the screen. It is almost always better for them to walk on from one side. If characters fly, a dramatic effect is to start by placing the character against the projection lamp for a large, diffused shadow. Then **move the puppet closer and closer** to the screen until its shadow is the same size as the puppet.

- **Make sure that the puppet stick is long enough** so that the puppeteer's hand does not show on the screen.

- **Place the puppet screen on a table** high enough so that puppeteers can sit comfortably underneath it without their heads getting in the way of the overhead projector light. Leave the area under the table exposed during rehearsal so the instructors can see what is happening behind the scenes and more effectively guide backstage traffic flow. Cover the table with bulletin board paper or a tablecloth for a more finished appearance during the performance.

- **Block out the puppet's movements much as is done in a play.** For shadow puppetry, you may have to orchestrate how the puppeteers move onstage as well as how the puppeteers move backstage. Set up a "waiting area" on either side (refer to page 177) where puppeteers can wait until they are needed. Choreograph backstage movements. Sometimes the person who made a puppet does not need to be the person who operates the puppet. Consider strategies to facilitate the least amount of backstage chaos.

- **Rehearse all scene changes.** These transitional times are often overlooked during the rehearsal process, but there is significant backstage movement during a scene change. Rehearse scene changes as if they are additional scenes in the play. Work out a cue between the scenery operator and the puppeteers to minimize the length of a scene change.

- Puppets are two-dimensional. **Try to avoid having them turn around while on stage.**

- **Try to have puppets react** to what is being said by gently tipping the body as if to nod or gently shaking the body to disagree. Small and gentle movements are better than larger, jerky movements.

- **Decide how the performance will end.** Will puppeteers come from behind the screen, stand in a line, and take a bow? Who will lead the bow? Will they show their puppets?

■ STEP TEN: REFLECT AND REVISE

One effective way to lead student reflection about a shadow puppet project is to videotape a rehearsal. As students review their work, encourage them to use the performance reflection sheet (see page 114) to plan improvements.

■ STEP ELEVEN: PERFORM

Invite parents, other classes, and administrators to the final performance. Invite students to welcome the audience and explain the project's process and what was learned.

■ STEP TWELVE: REFLECT AND EVALUATE

After the audience has left, gather the class to discuss successes and lessons learned. Ask how the project could be improved for the next group and, as in the sandwiching technique (chapter 5), which parts of the project should be kept for next time. Ask students to self-evaluate and complete the instructor evaluation.

■ LESSON PLAN IDEAS

Shadow puppetry is so rich and flexible it can be used to enhance nearly any curricular area. Some suggestions are discussed below.

Music

Pictures at an Exhibition. Modest Mussorgsky created music based on a walk through a fictional art gallery. Student groups each select one movement of *Pictures* and create a shadow tableau to represent it.

Library Skills

Dewey Decimal System. Divide the class into 10 groups for the 10 major classifications (the "hundreds") of the Dewey Decimal System. Ask each group to create a series of images that represents what can be found in that section.

Book care. Ask students to create puppet skits showing good and bad book care behaviors.

Science

Little Blue and Little Yellow (Leo Lionni). Use puppets made of blue and yellow gel to retell Lionni's color-mixing story.

Metamorphosis/life cycles. Have students create a series of shadow puppets to illustrate a scientific change: the seed cycle, water cycle, or life-change cycle.

Ocean life. Research ocean life and prepare a shadow play voyage to the bottom of the ocean. What sound effects might help to create the atmosphere? Consider using waxed paper or colored theatrical gel for the sea.

Landforms. Assign each group a different landform (isthmus, peninsula, plateau, etc.). Students create scenery depicting the land form, then write an original script that takes place in that setting.

Shadow zoo. Turn the standard animal research project into a trip to a shadow zoo! Students work in pairs to research an assigned animal. One student acts as narrator, describing the animal, while the other shows it off behind the screen.

Solar system. Instead of creating a solar system of foam balls, use shadow puppets instead.

Social Studies

Field trip. After researching a world country, have student groups create a shadow "field trip" that introduces the audience to the major sites, features, and customs of that nation.

Biography. Divide the class into biography research teams. Ask students to create puppets and a script that succinctly describe the famous person and the high points of his or her achievements.

Ancient Egypt. Explore ancient Egypt by creating a page from the papyrus *Day of the Dead*. Create puppets for at least one row of hieroglyphic characters. Create a script in which each explains his or her importance. Use the Metropolitan Museum of Art's Ancient Egypt Web site (http://www.metmuseum.org/explore/newegypt/htm/wk_frame.htm) as a source for images and research explanation.

Mayan culture. Have groups research the ancient Mayans and create an original play featuring the architecture and myths of the period.

Historical period. Have students research a major episode of a historical period and create a shadow script and play that is either historical fiction, a documentary, or a biography. This project works particularly well for historical periods from the late 1800s on, for which photographic documentation is available. Researching through photographs is particularly satisfying to students. Use the lesson plan structure from chapter 9 for this project. For a sample rubric for this type of project, see page 195.

Name _____

Role(s) in Play _____

Rubric: Shadow Play Research Project

For each section, 1-5 points will be given; 5 points is the highest. The student will self-evaluate, and the teacher will also evaluate the project. The teacher gives the final grade.

	STUDENT SCORE (1-5)	TEACHER SCORE (1-5)
RESEARCH		
I began my research by reading an encyclopedia entry.		
I wrote at least two preliminary questions to share at our planning conference.		
I participated in a planning conference with my teammates and teacher/media specialist.		
We created a plan at the conference.		
My team used at least three online sources for research and printed them out.		
The sources we used were of high quality.		
I highlighted and took notes on my web printouts.		
TEAMING		
I worked well as a member of a team.		
Work was equally shared by all teammates.		
PROJECT		
Our script is historical fiction, a documentary, or a biography.		
Our script contains accurate facts and historical information.		
Our script has a logical sequence of events.		
Our script has good spelling, punctuation, and capitalization.		
Our script is neatly typed and follows script-writing conventions.		
Our bibliography is complete, neat, and typed.		
PRESENTATION		
We presented the play in a professional manner.		
The puppet silhouettes communicate information about the characters to the audience.		
There is a color backdrop or other scenery that creates an understandable setting.		
One person acts as the narrator; the other(s) is/are puppeteers or scenery operators.		
The audience does not see shadows of heads or hands on the screen.		
The puppets are sturdily constructed and move smoothly onscreen.		
SUBTOTAL:		
TOTAL POINTS (OUT OF 100):		

Language Arts

Itsy Bitsy Spider. After students research the body parts of a spider, have each create a spider shadow puppet. Groups of students go behind a long, rectangular screen. The rest of the class acts as the audience and sings the song while the puppeteers re-create the action with their puppets.

Chicka Chicka Boom Boom (Martin and Archimbault 1989). For a quick post-storytime activity, use alphabet puppets made from Ellison die cuts and cardstock paper.

Introduction to prepositions. Prepositions often describe relative location (on, off, over, under, through, etc.). To make this meaningful for students, divide the class into groups. Give each group three prepositions to illustrate via a shadow puppetry scene.

Cinderella stories. Many cultures have a version of the Cinderella story. Have groups select a Cinderella story from another culture, research the traditional homes, palaces, and clothing of that culture, then create a script.

The Very Hungry Caterpillar (Eric Carle 1979). Create puppets for this text after researching the life cycle of a butterfly. Carle's simple silhouettes are easily re-created by students. Use a hole punch to represent the caterpillar's bites.

The Very Quiet Cricket (Eric Carle 1990). This project is a great match to a first-grade curriculum about insects. In the media center, have students begin by researching an assigned insect from Pebble Books's Insects series in groups of three, creating a "field guide" with important information about the insect, as well as a sketch. In the classroom, students read Eric Carle's *The Very Quiet Cricket* with their teacher. Special attention is given to the way in which the characters' greetings ("Good morning!" "Good night!") signify the passing of a day. Using what they know about insects, the students identify which of Carle's characters is an insect and which is not. The noninsects are removed from the story and replaced with insects learned about during the research period. Each research group makes puppets representing their insect, using pipe cleaners for legs and antennae. Care is taken to ensure that the insects have six legs and the proper body parts. The script, created in advance by the instructors, is read by student narrators. A backstage circular pattern is rehearsed so that each group can "cycle" in front of the screen at the proper time. A long, rectangular screen helps with traffic flow.

Civics

Community helpers improvisation. Following research or interviews, students create puppets of community helpers and children. They then create scenes showing the community helpers in action.

Fire safety demonstration. Many early elementary students have a unit on fire safety. Have them demonstrate a safety tip by creating a brief shadow tableau.

CONCLUSION

Shadow puppetry is an elegant, expressive medium for demonstrating understanding. Inexpensive yet eye-popping, it connects to and infuses traditional curriculum with beauty and aesthetic appeal.

REFERENCES

Carle, Eric. 1979. *The Very Hungry Caterpillar.* New York: Collins. unpaged. ISBN 0529007754; 0529007762 (lib. bdg.).

Carle, Eric. 1990. *The Very Quiet Cricket.* New York: Philomel. unpaged. ISBN 0399218858.

Fontichiaro, Kristin. 2006. "Using Shadow Puppets to Motivate and Showcase Student Learning." *School Library Media Activities Monthly* XXIII(1) (September): 27–30.

Honey, James A. [1910]. "Cloud Eating." In *South-African Folk-Tales.* Available at http://www.sacred-texts.com/afr/saft/sft27.htm (accessed January 15, 2007).

Lionni, Leo. 1994, 1959. *Little Blue and Little Yellow: A Story for Pippo and Ann and Other Children.* 1st Mulberry ed. New York: Mulberry. unpaged. ISBN 0688132855 (pbk.).

Martin, Bill, and John Archambault. 1989. *Chicka Chicka Boom Boom.* Illustrated by Lois Ehlert. New York: Simon & Schuster. 36pp. ISBN 1559245778.

Metropolitan Museum of Art. *Art of Ancient Egypt: Works of Art.* Available at http://www.metmuseum.org/explore/newegypt/htm/wk_frame.htm (accessed January 15, 2007).

Stanford University Libraries. *Copyright and Fair Use.* Available at http://fairuse.stanford.edu/Copyright_and_Fair_Use_Overview/chapter9/index.html (accessed January 15, 2007).

Wisniewski, David, and Donna Wisniewski. 1997. *Worlds of Shadow: Teaching with Shadow Puppetry.* Englewood, CO: Teacher Ideas Press. 225pp. ISBN 1563084503.

ADDITIONAL RESOURCES

AIMS Multimedia. *Indonesia.* 1999. Available at http://www.unitedstreaming.com (accessed January 15, 2007).

Champlin, Connie. *Storytelling with Puppets.* Chicago: American Library Association, 1985. 293pp. ISBN 0838904211 (paper).

Chorao, Kay. *Shadow Night: A Picture Book with Shadow Play.* 1st ed. New York: Dutton, 2001. unpaged. ISBN 052546685.

Codell, Esme Raji *How to Get Your Child to Love Reading: For Ravenous and Reluctant Readers Alike.* 1st ed. Chapel Hill, NC: Algonquin Books, 2003. 531pp. ISBN 1565123085.

Currell, David. *Learning with Puppets.* Boston: Plays, 1980. 207pp. ISBN 0823802507.

Discover Indonesia. *Wayang Kulit.* 2005. Available at http://discover-indo.tierranet. com/wayang.html (accessed January 15, 2007).

Discovery Channel School. *Bali: Land of a Thousand Temples.* 1997. Available at http://www.unitedstreaming.com (accessed January 15, 2007).

Fleischman, Paul. *Shadow Play.* Illustrated by by Eric Beddows. New York: Harper & Row, 1990. 33pp. ISBN 0060218657.

Lade, Roger. *The Most Excellent Book of How to be a Puppeteer.* London: Aladdin/ Watts, 1996. 32pp. ISBN 0749624779.

Old Sturbridge Village Kids Club. *Make a Shadow Puppet Theatre!* Available at http://www.osv.org/kids/crafts2.htm (accessed January 15, 2007).

Politi, Leo. *Mr. Fong's Toy Shop.* New York: Charles Scribner's Sons, 1978. unpaged. ISBN 0684155834 (lib. bdg.).

Robson, Denny, and Bailey, Vanessa. *Shadow Theater.* Rainy Days series. New York: Gloucester Press, 1991. 32pp. ISBN 0531172708.

Sheppard, Tim. *Tim Sheppard's Story Links.* Available at http://www.timsheppard. co.uk/story/storylinks.html (accessed January 15, 2007).

United Learning. *Stage One Science: Light and Color.* 1994. Available at http://www.unitedstreaming.com (accessed January 15, 2007).

Watson, N. Cameron. *The Little Pigs' Puppet Book.* Boston: Little, Brown, 1990. 32pp. ISBN 0316924687 (lib. bdg.).

Wright, Lyndie. *Puppets.* Illustrated by Chris Fairclough. New York: Franklin Watts, 1989. 48pp. ISBN 0531106357.

Young, Ed, and Hilary Beckett. *The Rooster's Horns: A Chinese Puppet Play to Make and Perform.* New York: Collins+World, 1978. unpaged. ISBN 0529054469; 0529054477 (lib. bdg.).

The author thanks Gail Trapp Bohner and Brenda Gluth of the Brighton (Michigan) Public Schools for their collaboration on past shadow puppet projects. Thank you to Sarah Credo for the collaborative project based on *The Very Quiet Cricket.*

The lesson plan for *The Very Quiet Cricket* previously appeared in the September 2006 issue of *School Library Media Activities Monthly.*

Part IV

Advocacy

Chapter 11
Advocating for Arts-Infused Curriculum in the Media Center

As this book comes to its conclusion, it is important to reflect on the importance of promoting and advocating for arts-based work in the school library media center. Many school administrators and parents may not realize the value of arts education. A strong advocacy program shows the learning embedded in what seems to be just *fun*.

Traditionally, librarians—especially school librarians—have not been trained to advocate for their programs and instructional methods. However, in the twenty-first century, this is an urgent matter. It is important that parents and decision makers be aware of the complex, deep-thinking work in which students engage when they are in the media center. Many of these influential adults grew up in schools where the school library was "just a place to get books," not a place to stretch the mind and prepare for the modern workforce. Well-informed stakeholders can work to secure a bright future for school libraries.

Some simple advocacy activities can raise the profile of the media center and share the good work being done by students. Toward this goal:

- **Keep a camera at the ready to capture students' "aha" moments.** Assign older students to be "documentarians" for class projects. Publish the photos in school newsletters, on the library Web site, or in slideshows.

- **Profile student projects in the school newsletter, on the school Web site, and on displays both inside and outside the media center.** Use mainstream vocabulary that is readily understood instead of "information literacy talk" that may not be understood by most people.

- **Promote student work using the school's PowerPoint™ broadcast.** Many schools are equipped to run a continuous PowerPoint presentation of announcements and photos. Be sure media center events are documented in this slideshow.

- **Videotape and share student projects.** Use software like iMovie™ or Windows MovieMaker™ to edit video and export it into digital format. Play the videos at Open House, Curriculum Night, or in the hallway outside the media center. Post them online so school board members, out-of-town parents, and voters have access. Export them into DVD format using iDVD™ or a PC DVD-authoring program. If funding permits, distribute copies of the DVD at a PTA meeting. Create a portable video portfolio by exporting iMovie files into iPod™ format or by placing exported MovieMaker files onto newer-model handheld devices such as PDAs or Palms™. Loan this portable video portfolio to an administrator so he or she can share it at an administrative team meeting. All administrators want to share good news about their school. Because many building offices are in the front of the school, and many media centers are in the heart of the school, they may not be regular witnesses to the positive outcomes of the media center. Bringing these achievements to administrators' attention helps them share the excitement with others.

- **Create artist statements that describe the work.** Take a tip from art teachers, who write a few paragraphs describing the inspiration and skills used by their students and post it alongside the student work. Post similar artist statements about the students' performing arts work next to online files or video monitors.

- **Use podcasting software** to capture students interviewing one another about what they learned during a project. Free software like Audacity (http://audacity.sourceforge.net) can record the interviews. The resulting files can be posted to the Web. Alternatively, Windows Media Player™ or iTunes™ can convert the files into audio CDs. Throw a launch party for families and the community.

- **Introduce live performances with an explanation of the skills developed by students.** Be sure to mention the higher-level thinking and concentration skills needed! Keep your school principal, district administration, and school board in mind if hosting a public event. Most love to be affiliated with an upbeat, positive event and may want to greet parents.

- **Encourage students to develop their own artist statements.** When students present small group or individual projects in performance, encourage them to speak for themselves about the process and lessons learned.

- **Invite parents and decision makers to observe your classes.** Parents and school officials love to see students actively engaged in learning.

- **Create a one-page media center brochure** that lists the online subscription passwords, philosophy of the media center, explanation of the arts integration projects done, and summary of the media curriculum.

- **Create screensavers for all library computers that feature student work.** Free photo software like Picasa™ (http://picasa.google.com) and iPhoto™ (which comes free with new Mac computers) creates photo screensavers in moments. A more complex software like Photoshop™ or GIMP (a free download at http://www.theopencd.org/programs) will allow staff your students to layer text on top of the photos to describe the project and what was learned.

- **Create a circulation desk slideshow display** that outlines what the media center has to offer to the student and parent community. Use an outdated or donated computer and equip it with PowerPoint (or the free open source version, Impress, available at http://www.openoffice.org). Set the slideshow to "loop" so it runs continuously. The slide show can also contain examples of student work. Use foam board to create a colorful, artsy "frame" around the monitor.

- **Share lessons learned with other media specialists and teachers.** If a project has gone well, offer to share it at a staff meeting or media meeting. If not, invite your colleagues to help you brainstorm how to improve it for next time.

■ CONCLUSION

The arts have so much to offer to nurture the heart, soul, and mind of students. They motivate students to do good work and challenge them to produce creative works. Because the projects call on students to process information and create a new product, this instructional method is virtually plagiarism-free. Arts projects facilitate opportunities for team teaching and collaborative planning that are enjoyed by participants and audiences alike.

The lessons in this book are just the beginning. If something in this book works well for you, if it serves as a springboard for your own variations, or even if you have struggled and need some advice, drop me a line at learningalive@ gmail.com. Remember . . . the arts are collaborative. We all learn from each other.

Bibliography

AIMS Multimedia. *Part 5: Readers Theatre: Historical Fiction.* UnitedStreaming, 1990. Available at http://www.unitedstreaming.com (accessed January 15, 2007).

Americans for the Arts. *Highlights from Key National Research on Arts Education.* Available at http://www. Americansforthearts.org/public_awareness/articles/ 002.asp (accessed August 31, 2006).

Annenberg Media/Maryland Public Television. "Part 6: Dramatic Tableaux." *Making Meaning in Literature.* Available at http://www.learner.org/resources/ series169.html (accessed August 28, 2006).

Burton, Virginia Lee. *Mike Mulligan and His Steam Shovel.* 60th anniv. ed. Boston: Houghton Mifflin, 1999 (c1939). 44pp. ISBN 0395169615.

Carle, Eric. *The Very Hungry Caterpillar.* New York: Collins, 1979. unpaged. ISBN 0529007754; 0529007762 (lib. bdg.).

Carle, Eric. *The Very Quiet Cricket.* New York: Philomel, 1990. unpaged. ISBN 0399218858.

Deasy, Richard J., ed. *Critical Links: Learning in the Arts and Student Academic and Social Development.* Arts Education Partnership, 2002. Available at http://www.aep-arts.org/publications/info.htm?publication_id=10 (accessed February 12, 2007).

dePaola, Tomie. *The Legend of the Bluebonnet: An Old Tale of Texas.* New York: Putnam, 1983. 30pp. ISBN 0399209379; 0399209387 (pbk.)

Di Camillo, Kate. *The Mysterious Journey of Edward Tulane.* Cambridge, MA: Candlewick, 2006. 198pp. ISBN 0763625892.

Discovery Channel School. *Teacher to Teacher: Professional Development for Today's Classroom: Language Arts Volume II.* 2005. Available at http://www. unitedstreaming.com/ (accessed January 15, 2007).

Drucker, Malka, and Michael Halperin. *Jacob's Rescue: A Holocaust Story.* New York: Bantam Skylark, 1993. 117pp. ISBN 0553089765.

Eastman, P. D. *Are You My Mother?* New York: Random House, 1960.

Edwards, Pamela Duncan. *Gigi and Lulu's Gigantic Fight.* New York: Katherine Tegen Books, 2002. unpaged. ISBN 0060507535.

Epstein, Shira D. "Reimagining Literary Practices: Creating Living Midrash from Ancient Texts Through Tableau." *Journal of Jewish Education* 70(1/2) (Summer 2004).

Festival of Arts Web site. http://foapom.com (accessed August 28, 2006).

Fiske, Edward B., ed. *Champions of Change: The Impact of the Arts on Learning*. Arts Education Partnership and the President's Committee on Arts and Humanities, 1999. Available at http://www.aep-arts.org/publications.html (accessed August 31, 2006).

Fontichiaro, Kristin. "Drama Machines: Learning Alive!" *School Library Media Activities Monthly* 22(6) (February 2006): 29–31.

Fontichiaro, Kristin. "Using Shadow Puppets to Motivate and Showcase Student Learning." *School Library Media Activities Monthly* XXIII(1) (September 2006): 27–30.

Frank, Anne. *The Diary of a Young Girl: The Definitive Edition*. New York: Doubleday, 1995. 340pp. ISBN 0385473788; 038542695X.

Freeman, Judy. *Books Kids Will Sit Still For 3: A Read-Aloud Guide*. Westport, Conn.: Libraries Unlimited, 2006. 915pp. ISBN 159158163X; 1591581648 (pbk).

Friedman, Thomas J. *The World Is Flat*. 1st ed. New York: Farrar, Straus & Giroux, 2005. 488pp. ISBN 0374292884.

Henkes, Kevin. *Lilly's Purple Plastic Purse*. New York: Greenwillow, 1996. unpaged. ISBN 068812898X (lib. bdg.)

Honey, James A. "Cloud Eating." In *South-African Folk-Tales*. Available at http://www.sacred-textsts.com/afr/saft/sft27.htm (accessed January 15, 2007).

Kelner, Lenore Blank, and Rosalind Flynn *A Dramatic Approach to Reading Comprehension*. Portsmouth, NH: Heinemann, 2006. 229pp. ISBN 0325007942.

Kennedy Center. *Teaching Tableau*. 2007. Available at http://artsedge. kennedy-center. org/content/3933/index.html (accessed January 16, 2007).

Layne, Sean. *Living Pictures: A Theatrical Technique for Learning Across the Curriculum*. Washington, DC: Kennedy Center, 2001–2002. (VHS video). Available for purchase at http://www.kennedy-center.org/education/pdot/livingpictures.

Lionni, Leo. *Little Blue and Little Yellow: A Story for Pippo and Ann and Other Children*. 1st Mulberry ed. New York: Mulberry, 1994, 1959. unpaged. ISBN 0688132855 (pbk.).

Lister, Mary. *The Winter King and the Summer Queen*. Illustrated by Diana Mayo. Cambridge, MA: Barefoot Books, 2002. unpaged. ISBN 1841483575.

Martin, Bill, and John Archambault. *Chicka Chicka Boom Boom*. Illustrated by Lois Ehlert. New York: Simon & Schuster, 1989. 36pp. ISBN 1559245778.

McMaster, Jennifer Catney. "'Doing' Literature: Using Drama to Build Literacy." *The Reading Teacher* 51(7) (1998): 574–580.

Metropolitan Museum of Art. *Art of Ancient Egypt: Works of Art*. Available at http://www.metmuseum.org/explore/newegypt/htm/wk_frame.htm (accessed January 15, 2007).

National Archives Education Department. *Teaching with Documents: Lesson Plans.* Available at http://www.archives.gov/education/lessons/ (accessed August 28, 2006).

National Governors' Association. *The Impact of Arts Education on Workforce Preparation.* Available at http://www.nga.org/Files/pdf/050102ARTSED.pdf (accessed August 31, 2006).

Navarro, Mireya. "The Tableau Vivant Is Alive and Well and Living in Laguna Beach." *New York Times* (online), August 1, 2006.

O'Dell, Scott. *Island of the Blue Dolphins.* Boston: Houghton Mifflin, 1990, c1960. 181pp. ISBN 039553680.

Opp-Beckman, Leslie. "Tongue Twisters." *ESL PIZZAZ!* 2004. Available at http://darkwing.uoregon.edu/~leslieob/twisters.html (accessed August 10, 2006).

Oreck, Barry. "Talent Assessment Process." *Teaching Artist Journal* 3(4) (2006): 220–227.

Pacific Resources for Learning. *Telling Stories: Using Drama and Multimedia with ESL Students.* Available at http://www.prel.org/esltrategies/drama.html (accessed August 14, 2006).

Pink, Daniel H. *A Whole New Mind: Moving from the Information Age to the Conceptual Age.* New York: Riverhead Books, 2005. 260pp. ISBN 1573223085.

Rivera, Diego. *Detroit Industry.* Fresco, 1932–1933 (Detroit Institute of Arts). Available at http://www.dia.org/collections/AmericanArt/33.10.html (accessed January 15, 2007).

Spolin, Viola. *Improvisation for the Theater: A Handbook of Teaching and Directing Techniques.* 3d ed. Evanston, IL: Northwestern University Press, 1999. 412pp. ISBN 081014008X.

Staley, C. T. *Tongue Twister Database.* 2003. Available at http://www.geocities.com/athens/8136/tonguetwisters.html (accessed August 10, 2006).

Stanford University Libraries. *Copyright and Fair Use.* Available at http://fairuse.stanford.edu/Copyright_and_Fair_Use_Overview/chapter9/index.html (accessed January 15, 2007).

Sun, Ping-Yun. *Using Drama and Theatre to Promote Literacy Development: Some Basic Classroom Applications.* The Clearinghouse on Reading, English, and Communication Digest no. 187. Available at http://reading.indiana.edu/ieo/digests/d187.html (accessed August 14, 2006).

Thomas, Mark. *American Business History: Images.* Available at http://faculty.virginia.edu/hius341/images (accessed August 23, 2006).

Vail, Rachel. *Sometimes I'm Bombaloo.* New York: Scholastic, 2002. unpaged. ISBN 0439087554.

Walter P. Reuther Library, Wayne State University. *The Faces of Detroit.* Available at http://www.reuther.wayne.edu/faces/assemblyline.html (accessed August 23, 2006).

Wilhelm, Jeffrey D. *Action Strategies for Deepening Comprehension.* New York: Scholastic Professional, 2002. 192pp. ISBN 0439218578.

Wisniewski, David, and Donna Wisniewski. *Worlds of Shadow: Teaching with Shadow Puppetry.* Englewood, CO: Teacher Ideas Press, 1997. 225pp. ISBN 1563084503.

Woodson, Jacqueline. *Show Way.* Illustrated by Hudson Talbott. New York: G. P. Putnam, 2005. unpaged. ISBN 0399239496.

Index

Children's books and folktales are included in the author/illustrator/title index.

Author/Illustrator/Title Index

This index includes authors, illustrators, and titles of children's books and folktales; other works appear in the main index.

About the Author

KRISTIN FONTICHIARO is an elementary media specialist in Michigan. She has been a classroom teacher at the elementary, middle, and senior high school levels and an arts educator.